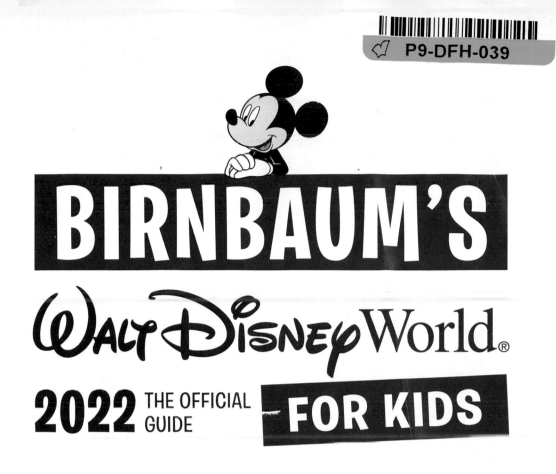

BIRNBAUM'S

Walt Disney World®

2022 THE OFFICIAL GUIDE — FOR KIDS

Wendy Lefkon EDITORIAL DIRECTOR

Jill Safro EDITOR

Jessica Ward CONTRIBUTING EDITOR

Jennie Hess CONTRIBUTING EDITOR

Alexandra Mayes Birnbaum CONSULTING EDITOR

Disney

EDITIONS

LOS ANGELES • NEW YORK

For Steve, who made all of this possible.

ISBN 978-1-368-06246-6
FAC-034274-21218
First Edition, September 2021
10 9 8 7 6 5 4 3 2 1

Printed in the United States of America

An enormous debt of gratitude is owed to Bruce Steele, Jerry Gonzalez, Jennifer Eastwood, Monica Vasquez, Lindsay Broderick, Gegham Vardanyan, Betty Avila, Marybeth Tregarthen, Geoffrey Cook, Steven Miller, Elisabeth Hurkes, Terry Brinkoetter, Jackie Vernon, Andrea Wolowitz, and Karen McClintock for making this book possible.

Other 2022 Birnbaum's Official Disney Guide:
Walt Disney World

Contents

 4 YOU'RE GOING TO DISNEY WORLD!

Plan, pack, and party as the countdown to your vacation officially begins.

 16 MAGIC KINGDOM

Read how to zoom through space, fly with Peter Pan, become a pirate, and see Mickey Mouse in the most magical place in the World.

 52 EPCOT

Discover the Disney version of tomorrow, take a high-flying world tour, ride a *Frozen* attraction, and see Anna and Elsa.

 79 DISNEY'S HOLLYWOOD STUDIOS

Step into imaginary worlds from TV and movies — *Toy Story*, *Star Wars*, The Muppets, and more — and enjoy attractions with a showbiz twist.

 101 DISNEY'S ANIMAL KINGDOM

Want to visit real wild animals? Fly on the back of a dragon-like banshee? Or take a wild, watery raft ride? This chapter tells you how.

121 EVERYTHING ELSE IN THE WORLD

Learn what's at Walt Disney World besides theme parks — water parks, mini-golf courses, and tons of other fun spots. There are awesome hotels and hundreds of restaurants, too.

 142 MAGICAL MEMORIES

Save the precious memories of your Disney trip before you start planning the next one!

© Disney

You're Going to
DISNEY WORLD!

When you first heard the news, you could not believe your ears. Could it be true? Were you really going on a vacation to Walt Disney World? Well, believe it or not, it's true! Before you know it, you will be in the sunny state of Florida. It's the home of Walt Disney World and the most famous mouse on planet Earth. (Big hint: His name starts with M.)

If you have ever been there, you already know that it is a mighty big place with lots to do. In fact, there is so much going on that it can get a little confusing. That's where this book comes in handy. It describes everything in the World, from the Magic Kingdom theme park to treasure hunts with pirate pals. And it's filled with advice from kids like you.

There is no right or wrong way to read this book. You can start on the first page and read straight through to the end. Or you can skip around, read your favorite parts first, and come back to the rest later.

No matter what you do, one thing is for sure: When you are done, you will be a true-blue Walt Disney World expert. Soon folks may start asking YOU for advice on how to have the most awesome vacation at Walt Disney World!

Pack a Pen and Take Me Along With You

Don't leave this book behind when you head for the parks. It is full of tips and information that you will want to remember. There are pages for photos and autographs, too — don't forget to bring a pen and your camera. Here are some ways to use this book while visiting the wonderful world of Disney:

Track Your Trip

Each time you check out a Disney World attraction, check it off in this book. Then you'll know what's left to see on your next visit.

We're Warning You!

Disney rides are full of surprises. That's part of what makes them so much fun. But not everyone likes surprises. So if things like loud noises or wild turns scare you, look at the book's attraction reaction warnings before you go on each ride. That way, the only surprises you come across will be good ones!

Find the Fastpass

Would you like to go to the front of the line at theme park rides? You can if Disney offers its Fastpass+ system during your visit and you have **Fastpass+** reservations. Here's how it works: Reserve a Fastpass with the My Disney Experience app or website (ask a parent for help). You may also get a same-day Fastpass at a station in each park — get there early! Visit the attraction at your assigned time, and soon you should be on the ride. Will Fastpass+ be offered during your WDW visit? Ask a parent to visit *disneyworld.com* to find out.

Search for Hidden Mickeys

Disney Imagineers have hidden images of Mickey Mouse all over Walt Disney World. (Many look like the three connected circles that form Mickey's head.) You might see them in shadows, lights, drawings, or even in the clouds at some attractions. Look in this book for each **HIDDEN MICKEY ALERT!** to find a clue. Keep track of the number of Hidden Mickeys that you discover. When your Walt Disney World trip is over, write that number on page 149 of this book's Magical Memories section.

Read about Walt Disney World's 50th anniversary on page 158!

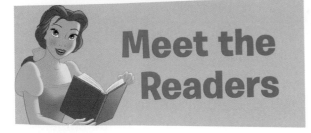

Meet the Readers

What do the kids who helped with this book have in common? They love Walt Disney World! How do we know? They told us so! Every kid who wrote to us last year received a survey form. The surveys came back filled with opinions about Walt Disney World. The forms also helped us find out about readers' interests and hobbies.

What did we learn? For starters, a lot of you enjoy reading, writing, playing sports, making music, and computers. You also like drawing, singing, and dancing. Your top Disney hotels are Port Orleans Riverside, Polynesian Village, Beach Club, and Animal Kingdom Lodge. Not all of you are crazy about dark or scary rides. But wild rides like Expedition Everest, Space Mountain, and Big Thunder Mountain are at the top of your list. You think Blizzard Beach is the perfect place to splash around. And when you can't find a Mickey Mouse ice cream bar to snack on, you love popcorn, Mickey-shaped pretzels, a turkey leg, or a frozen pineapple treat called Dole Whip. Yum!

To everyone who filled out a survey form, THANK YOU! This book could not have been written without you. And feel free to write again. We love to hear from our readers!

— Jill Safro, Editor

Mickey is Number One!

It's probably not a surprise to hear that Mickey Mouse is the most popular Disney character with readers. And his best girl, Minnie, is in second place. But who would have guessed that Goofy would be a close third? Gawrsh! Rounding out the top five faves are Donald and Pluto. Who is your favorite? Let us know!

The Magic Kingdom Rules!

More than half of our readers chose the Magic Kingdom as their favorite theme park. What's yours?

MAGIC KINGDOM **61%**
ANIMAL KINGDOM **10%**
EPCOT **16%**
DISNEY'S HOLLYWOOD STUDIOS **13%**

You Love a Wild Ride!

We asked you what types of rides you like best. It turns out most of you like the twists and turns of thrill rides. What daredevils!

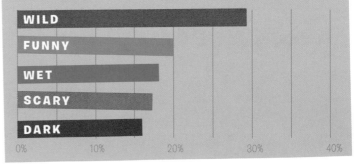

WILD
FUNNY
WET
SCARY
DARK

0%   10%   20%   30%   40%

Look for this Reader Pleaser stamp throughout the book. We've placed it by readers' favorite Disney World shows and attractions. If you'd like to vote for next year's Reader Pleasers, email us and we will send you a survey form. Our email address is listed in the orange box below.

READER TIP

Keep an eye out for this sign. Every time you spot one, you will find a great tip sent in by a reader. Do you have any Walt Disney World tips? We would love to hear them!

What do YOU Think?

Do you agree or disagree with any of the kids in this book? Tell us what you think! First, ask a parent for permission. Together you can send us an email about your Disney trip. Would you like us to send you a survey form? Just ask! The official email address for *Birnbaum's Walt Disney World for Kids* is below:

WDI.Birnbaum.Guides.For.Kids@disney.com

READER REVIEW

Every reader who was sent a survey also got an application to be a Birnbaum Ace Reporter. Some of their Reader Reviews appear next to the attraction descriptions in this book. Use the advice from the Ace Reporters to decide if an attraction is worth the wait or is one to skip!

AND THE WINNER IS . . .

One lucky Ace Reporter was picked at random to win a Disney prize. And the winner is . . . Kathleen from Normal, Illinois!

Kathleen is 13 years old. Her favorite Walt Disney World attractions are Avatar Flight of Passage and Na'vi River Journey. Who's on top of her favorite character list? Simba and Nala! Kathleen enjoys dancing, drawing, singing, and acting. She loves animals of all kinds — so Animal Kingdom is her favorite Disney park. And when it comes to Walt Disney World hotels, she's a big fan of Port Orleans Riverside.

Way to go, Kathleen! Thanks for your valuable input to the newest edition of *Birnbaum's Walt Disney World For Kids*.

PHOTO BY MIKE CARROLL

Meet the Editor

Hi. My name is Jill. I'm one of the big kids who helped put this book together. Mickey and Minnie helped us out, too!

Meet Walt Disney!

Walt came to think of Mickey Mouse as his own son.

Walt Disney was born in Illinois on December 5, 1901 — that's more than one hundred years ago. During his life and for all the years after, Walt Disney's company created famous cartoons, movies, theme parks, books, and toys (plus much more) for everyone to enjoy . . . but how did it all begin?

When Walt was a little boy, he would look up at the sky and imagine the clouds were animals. As the wind pushed a cloud, a pig would turn into a cow. Soon, the cow would become a chicken! It was then that young Walt realized that anything was possible with a little imagination.

But he knew that success would not come from daydreaming alone. Growing up on a farm had taught him the importance of hard work. And it's a good thing, because without Walt's hard work, we would never have met the most famous mouse in the world.

MAGICAL MILESTONES

1901
Walt Disney is born on December 5 in Chicago, Illinois.

1928
Walt creates Mickey Mouse. Mickey stars in the cartoon *Steamboat Willie*.

1937
Walt's animators finish *Snow White and the Seven Dwarfs*, one of the first full-length animated films.

1955
Walt's dream to make a family theme park comes true. Disneyland opens in Anaheim, California.

1971
Walt Disney World (sometimes called WDW) opens near Orlando, Florida.

1975
The first WDW roller coaster opens: Space Mountain!

1982
EPCOT opens at WDW.

A mouse is born

In 1928, Walt created a little cartoon mouse. (Walt almost named him Mortimer Mouse. Luckily, Lilly Disney convinced her husband to name him Mickey Mouse instead!) Mickey's first movie was a black-and-white cartoon called *Steamboat Willie*. It was an instant success. But one hit was not enough for its creator. Walt was always looking for new challenges.

In 1937, his company made one of the first full-length cartoon movies: *Snow White and the Seven Dwarfs*. Walt was proud that he had made a movie for everyone in the family to enjoy. Family was very important to Walt. Every Saturday, he would do something special with his two daughters. They often went to an amusement park. The kids loved it, but Walt was sad that there weren't any rides for parents. He thought, *I wish there were a place where children and grown-ups could have fun together.*

A dream is a wish your heart makes

Since a place like that didn't exist, Walt decided to build it. At first he was going to call it Mickey Mouse Park, but then he named it Disneyland. Disneyland opened in Anaheim,

***Steamboat Willie* was the first talking cartoon ever made.**

California, in 1955. Families traveled from around the world to visit it. Disneyland was so popular that Walt's new dream was to build a bigger park: Disney World. He must have wished upon a star — because his dream came true.

Mickey's birthday is NOVEMBER 18.® When is yours?

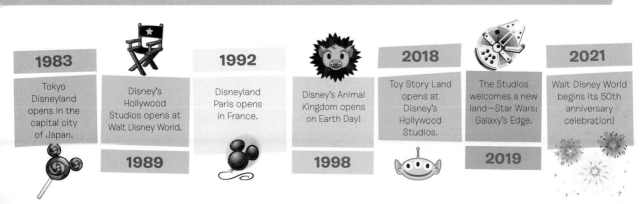

1983 — Tokyo Disneyland opens in the capital city of Japan.

1989 — Disney's Hollywood Studios opens at Walt Disney World.

1992 — Disneyland Paris opens in France.

1998 — Disney's Animal Kingdom opens on Earth Day!

2018 — Toy Story Land opens at Disney's Hollywood Studios.

2019 — The Studios welcomes a new land—Star Wars: Galaxy's Edge.

2021 — Walt Disney World begins its 50th anniversary celebration!

What a Wonderful World!

Walt Disney loved dreaming up stories to tell and new ways to tell them. After he died, his brother Roy kept one of his biggest dreams alive. He made sure Walt's special "world" was built just the way Walt had imagined it. Roy even insisted that it be called Walt Disney World, so everyone would know it had been his brother's dream.

Walt Disney World officially opened in Florida on October 1, 1971. Since then, millions of people have stopped in for a visit. Some people come to Walt Disney World for a day, but most stay a little longer. There is just so much to see and do.

Pick a theme park, any theme park

The most famous part of Walt Disney World is the **Magic Kingdom**. It's home to Cinderella Castle, Space Mountain, and those rascally Pirates of the Caribbean. It is also where you can have an adventure with Peter Pan or Winnie the Pooh. Kids of all ages can't get enough of this happy place. Of course, there are three other theme parks to enjoy.

EPCOT is a place of wonder and discovery. Here you can search for Nemo at The Seas with Nemo and Friends, ride the frosty Frozen Ever

Disney's Animal Kingdom celebrates the beauty of nature and the creatures that live in it. It got off to a roaring start in 1998. The park has what it takes to make any kid's day: an African safari ride with wild animals, dinosaurs that seem real, a roller coaster adventure with an abominable snowman, and a funny 3-D movie about insects.

Chill out!

After attraction, and see Anna and Elsa. It is also a great place to drive a speedy new car and go on a "world tour." Different countries have shops, restaurants, and attractions inside this park. EPCOT opened in 1982.

Are you a showbiz fan? If so, you will get a kick out of **Disney's Hollywood Studios** theme park. It's filled with attractions that were inspired by movies and TV shows. You can enter a cartoon world at Mickey and Minnie's Runaway Railway and play in Andy's backyard at Toy Story Land. Guests can fly a spaceship in an area called Star Wars: Galaxy's Edge. And The Twilight Zone Tower of Terror scares everybody silly. Disney's Hollywood Studios opened in 1989.

Need to cool off on a hot Florida day? You can make a splash at a Disney water park. Between **Typhoon Lagoon** and **Blizzard Beach**, it's almost impossible to stay dry. Each one has slippery slides, tube rides, and some very cool pools.

But wait — there's more! Walt Disney World also has boats, bikes, and even horses to ride. It has hundreds of restaurants, shops, and other places to explore. In fact, no matter how many times you visit, there is always something new to see. Will Walt Disney World ever be finished? Not as long as there is imagination left in the world. And that's exactly how Walt would have wanted it.

Getting Ready to Go

Planning a vacation to Walt Disney World can be lots of fun. But it is not as easy as it sounds. There are so many choices to make! Which parks should you visit? What should you pack? And where can you meet your favorite Disney characters?

This book should answer many of your questions and help plan your Disney vacation. Remember: It's never too early to get started!

MAKE A SIMPLE SCHEDULE

Did you know that there are more than 300 shows and attractions at Walt Disney World? It could take weeks to see them all. And most people don't have weeks to spend on vacation. That's why it's important to make a schedule before you leave home. Without it, you might miss some of the rides you want to try the most.

What you will need

Paper, a pencil, and this book!

What to do

1. Write **Magic Kingdom** at the top of a piece of paper.

2. Look at the Magic Kingdom chapter. Every time you see an attraction that sounds like fun, write its name on the paper.

3. When you have finished the chapter, look over your list. Then put a star next to your favorite attractions. These are your "must-sees."

4. Now make a schedule for each of the other theme parks you plan to visit.

5. Don't forget to take your Simple Schedules when you visit the parks!

Learn the Disney Lingo

AUDIO-ANIMATRONICS: Life-like robots, from birds and dinosaurs to movie stars and presidents. They seem real — but they're not.

CAST MEMBER: A Disney worker.

CIRCLE-VISION 360: A movie that surrounds you. The screens form a circle.

GUIDEMAP: A theme park map that also describes attractions, shops, restaurants, and entertainment.

IMAGINEER: A creative person who designs Disney shows and attractions.

MAGICBAND: A wrist band that can serve as a park ticket and WDW hotel-room key.

Save Room for Souvenirs

When you pack for your trip, make sure you prepare for the weather. Believe it or not, it gets chilly in Florida, especially in the winter. But the summer can be sizzling hot! It's usually warm during the rest of the year. Layers are a good idea, so you can take something off if you get hot. Remember to pack clothes and shoes that are lightweight and comfortable — since you'll do a lot of walking at the parks. And don't overstuff your suitcase. You may need room for the goodies you gather at Walt Disney World. What else should you bring? That's up to you! Here's a short list to help you get started:

- A sweatshirt or sweater
- Comfy sneakers or shoes
- Face coverings and hand sanitizer
- Shorts and pants
- Long sleeved and short-sleeved shirts
- A hat and sunglasses
- A swimsuit
- Pajamas
- Sunscreen
- Bug spray

Learn More about Walt Disney World

This book is filled with information, but there's another way to learn about Walt Disney World — the Internet. With a parent's permission you can use the (free) **My Disney Experience** mobile app or website, or visit **www.disneyworld.com**. If you have a question and don't have access to the Internet, write to:

Walt Disney World
P.O. Box 10000
Lake Buena Vista, FL 32830

Countdown to
Walt Disney World!

Take a look at a calendar. On which day does your Walt Disney World vacation begin? Once you find it, count back 10 days — that's the day you can start this special countdown.

To do it, draw a circle around the number for each day as it arrives. Then try the daily activity. Be sure to ask a grown-up for help. You can make up your own special activities, too!

10 DAYS TO GO

Start to plan a Disney party. Choose some of your favorite snacks for the menu. Who is on your guest list?

9 DAYS TILL DISNEY

Get to work on your Magic Kingdom Simple Schedule. (Read page 12 to learn how.) Which attractions do you want to visit first?

8 DAYS LEFT

Make a list with addresses of people you want to send postcards to.

7 DAYS . . .

Have you finished making your Magic Kingdom schedule yet? It's time to start your EPCOT Simple Schedule. Which attractions do you think sound best?

6 DAYS AND COUNTING

Make some Mouse ears! Tape strips of paper to make a loop big enough to fit around your head. Then cut out two circles and tape them to the front of the loop. Make a pair for everyone invited to your party.

5 DAYS MORE

Plan your Disney's Hollywood Studios Simple Schedule. And start packing! (Flip to page 13 for packing tips.)

4 DAYS NOW!

Get some popcorn and watch a favorite Disney movie with your family. Which flick did you pick? What movie do you want to watch next?

3 DAYS — IT WILL BE SOON!

Spend some time on your Animal Kingdom Simple Schedule tonight. Which theme park do you hope to visit first?

2 DAYS — JUST 2!

It's Disney dinner time! Set the table to look festive for your celebration. Be sure to share your park schedules with your family. Remember to wear your Mouse ears!

1 DAY LEFT — YIPPEE!

Don't stay up too late — tomorrow is the BIG DAY!

TODAY IS THE DAY!

Month / Day / Year

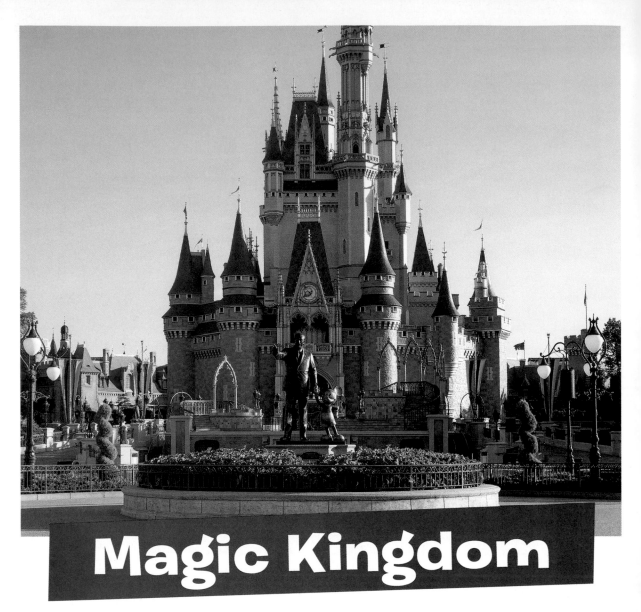

Magic Kingdom

When most people hear the words "Walt Disney World," they think of Cinderella Castle, Space Mountain, and Mickey Mouse. They're all in the Magic Kingdom, along with much more. That is why so many kids say the Magic Kingdom is the most special part of Walt Disney World.

You can spend lots of time exploring its six lands — Main Street, U.S.A., Adventureland, Frontierland, Liberty Square, Fantasyland, and Tomorrowland. This chapter will help you decide which shows and attractions you want to see first. After you read it, flip back to page 12. It lists tips on how to make a simple Magic Kingdom schedule. That way you can organize your park visit and avoid wasting time. If you're lucky, you will get to end the day by watching a fireworks show. That's Disney's way of giving guests a kiss good night.

N

FANTASYLAND

27

24

29

25 26

28

21

38

LIBERTY SQUARE

23 18

22

30

20

16

19

33

14 9 13

12

FRONTIERLAND

17 15

34

10 11

8

36 32 31

7

35

6

TOMORROWLAND

4

5

37

ADVENTURELAND

MAIN STREET, U.S.A.

3

2

1

MONORAIL STATION

DISNEY RESORT
BUS FACILITY

BOAT LAUNCH

FERRY BOAT LANDING

MAIN STREET, U.S.A.

1. Main Street Vehicles
2. Walt Disney World Railroad Station
3. Town Square Theater

ADVENTURELAND

4. Jungle Cruise
5. Pirates of the Caribbean
6. Swiss Family Treehouse
7. The Enchanted Tiki Room
8. The Magic Carpets of Aladdin

FRONTIERLAND

9. Big Thunder Mountain Railroad
10. Country Bear Jamboree
11. Frontierland Shootin' Arcade
12. Splash Mountain
13. Rafts to Tom Sawyer Island
14. Walt Disney World Railroad Station

LIBERTY SQUARE

15. The Hall of Presidents
16. The Haunted Mansion
17. Liberty Square Riverboat

FANTASYLAND

18. Prince Charming Regal Carrousel
19. It's a Small World
20. Mad Tea Party
21. The Many Adventures of Winnie the Pooh
22. Peter Pan's Flight
23. Mickey's PhilharMagic
24. Under the Sea —
    Journey of The Little Mermaid
25. Dumbo the Flying Elephant
26. The Barnstormer

27. Walt Disney World Railroad Station
28. Seven Dwarfs Mine Train
29. Enchanted Tales with Belle
30. Princess Fairytale Hall

TOMORROWLAND

31. Astro Orbiter
32. Buzz Lightyear's Space Ranger Spin
33. Tomorrowland Speedway
34. Space Mountain
35. Tomorrowland Transit Authority
    PeopleMover
36. Monsters, Inc. Laugh Floor
37. Walt Disney's Carousel of Progress
38. TRON Lightcycle/Run

Parade Route • • • • • • • • • •

Use this map to plan your visit to the Magic Kingdom!

Main Street, U.S.A.

PHOTO BY JILL SAFRO

Are you ready for some time traveling? You will do a lot of it in the Magic Kingdom. Four out of its six lands send you either back or forward in time. Main Street, U.S.A., is one of those lands. It was made to look like a small American town in the year 1900. (Some of it is based on the town Walt Disney grew up in: Marceline, Missouri.)

There are pretty lamp posts, horse-drawn trolleys, and many other touches that make the street charming. If you look both ways before crossing, you may notice a big difference between this Main Street and a real one: There's a castle at the end of it!

There are no major attractions here, but Main Street is a fun place to be. You can sink your teeth into a fresh-baked cupcake, hop aboard a fire truck, or watch a parade pass by.

Walt Disney World Railroad

Walt Disney loved trains. He even had a miniature one in his backyard that was big enough for him to ride on.

The Magic Kingdom trains are real locomotives that were built nearly a hundred years ago. A full trip takes about 20 minutes, but you can get on or off at any train station (Main Street, U.S.A., Frontierland, or Fantasyland).

What do most kids think about the Magic Kingdom's railroad? They love traveling by train. You get a great view of the park — plus a chance to rest your feet. The railroad may not be open in all of 2022.

READER REVIEW

There's no better cure for sore feet than a trip on the Walt Disney World Railroad. A friendly voice gives you information about the park, and there is a nice breeze. It's great for all ages.

— Emma (age 12), Deerfield, IL

HOT TIP!

The Main Street Vehicles were on pause in 2021 — but they are expected to return in 2022.

HIDDEN MICKEY ALERT!

Look by the railing around the statue of Walt Disney and Mickey Mouse at the end of Main Street — it makes a Mickey shadow!

Main Street Vehicles

The Walt Disney World Railroad isn't the only ride on Main Street, U.S.A. Horse-drawn trolleys, old-fashioned cars, and an antique fire engine make trips up and down the street early in the day.

You can climb aboard any one of these vehicles in Town Square or by Cinderella Castle. Each trip is one-way — you will be asked to hop off after the ride.

The vehicles do not run every day. Stop by the City Hall (on Main Street) to find out the schedule.

When the horses that pull the trolleys take a break, they can usually be found in the Car Barn. It's near the Emporium shop on Main Street. Stop by to say hello!

Adventureland

A trip to Adventureland is like a visit to a jungle. It has so many plants and trees that Tarzan would feel right at home. (Don't bother looking for him. He prefers his own treehouse to the one here. It's in Disneyland in California.)

As you can tell from the name of this land, the shows and attractions take you on exciting (and silly) adventures.

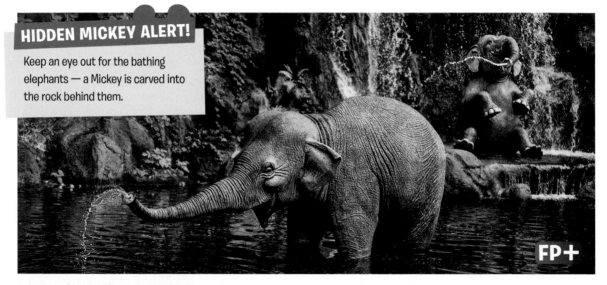

HIDDEN MICKEY ALERT!

Keep an eye out for the bathing elephants — a Mickey is carved into the rock behind them.

FP+

READER REVIEW

I like this ride because of all the corny jokes the captain tells. They are so funny! I liked the animals better when I was younger, but I still ride to hear those famous jokes!

— Shawn (age 12), York, PA

Jungle Cruise

It's a good thing elephants aren't shy. Otherwise, they might get upset when you watch them take a bath. That's just one of the interesting sights on the Jungle Cruise.

The voyage goes through the jungles of Africa and Asia. Along the way you see life-like zebras, giraffes, lions, hippos, snakes, and crocodiles. Don't worry — the only real animals in the ride are the human beings inside the boat.

The Jungle Cruise is usually very crowded — try to get there early in the morning. It's a good idea to ride during the day, when you can see everything. But if you would like a spookier ride, take the cruise at night.

Pirates of the Caribbean

Dead men tell no tales! That's the warning a pirate gives near the start of this attraction. Don't worry — this classic ride isn't going to hurt you. But there is a small dip and some dark scenes, so be prepared.

The journey takes place in a little boat. After floating through a cave…*BOOM!* You're in the middle of a pirate attack! Cannons blast while the song "Yo Ho, Yo Ho, a Pirate's Life for Me" plays in the background.

The pirates and animals look real. But they are Audio-Animatronics figures (kind of like robots). Look for a pirate with his leg hanging over a bridge — the leg is really hairy.

In case you didn't know: This is the attraction that inspired Disney's Pirates of the Caribbean movies. *Arrrrr!*

LOUD SCARY DARK

FP+

READER REVIEW

My favorite part of the ride is the lady chasing the pirates with a broom! My 6-year-old brother was afraid of the pirate battle. It's really not that scary, but it might be better for older kids.

— Conor (age 10), Cork, Ireland

HOT TIP!

Do you think you would make a good pirate? Find out by joining a special quest called A Pirate's Adventure — Treasure of the Seven Seas. You will use a map and a magic charm to help find treasure and keep enemies away! (This game may not be offered in all of 2022.)

FP+

HOT TIP!

Some riders can control how high or low the carpet flies. If you want this job, ask to sit in the front row of the carpet.

The Magic Carpets of Aladdin

If a genie offered to grant you some wishes, what would you wish for? To be a prince and win the heart of a princess? Maybe not. But that was Aladdin's wish — and thanks to his funny friend, Genie, his request came true (eventually).

You won't find a real genie at this ride, but you will get to take a high-flying trip on a magic carpet — much like Aladdin and Jasmine did in the movie.

The magic touch

This attraction is a bit like Dumbo the Flying Elephant in Fantasyland — riders use joysticks to control the flight. Also like Dumbo, these magic carpets really soar. Beware of the golden camel. It likes to spit at Magic Kingdom guests!

A whole new world

Kids who visit Adventureland may notice that the area has a special look. The shops and decorations make it look like the busy marketplace of Agrabah from *Aladdin*. You might even see characters from the movie during your visit. They love to pose for photos — so have your camera or mobile phone ready.

Swiss Family Treehouse

Before he wrote a book called *The Swiss Family Robinson*, Johann Wyss and his kids imagined what it would be like for their family to be stranded on an island. Together they came up with lots of crazy adventures for the Robinsons. They survive a shipwreck, fight off pirates, and build the most awesome treehouse in the world.

Walt Disney Productions made a movie based on the book in 1960. The Swiss Family Treehouse in Adventureland looks just like the treehouse in the film. In it, you climb a staircase to many different levels. Each room has lots to see. The tree looks very real, but it is not. It has 300,000 plastic leaves, and concrete roots.

HOT TIP!

The Magic Kingdom is famous for its fireworks shows. And one of the coolest places to watch is from the top of the Swiss Family Treehouse. Even when there's no show, this spot gives you a great view of Cinderella Castle. Be sure to check it out.

HIDDEN MICKEY ALERT!

Find the stone seating area outside the Swiss Family Treehouse. Then look at it very closely. It has two Hidden Mickeys on it!

SUPER SPLASH ZONES

There are lots of ways to make a splash at the Magic Kingdom. In Adventureland, look for a group of tiki statues and a golden camel near Swiss Family Treehouse. They're ready to cool you off with a squirt of water. If that's not enough watery fun, head to Casey Junior Splash and Soak Station in Fantasyland. It's splashy fun for everyone.

![Walt Disney's Enchanted Tiki Room sign]

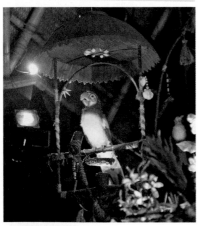

Walt Disney's Enchanted Tiki Room

Birds rule at this attraction. They also sing and crack lots of jokes. If you have been here before, you may know José, Michael, Fritz, and Pierre. They've been singing old favorites like "The Tiki, Tiki, Tiki Room" for 50 years.

So what makes this tiki room enchanted? We already know that the birds all sing — but so do the flowers! In fact, even the totem poles get in on the act. The show happens all around you, so don't forget to look up and behind you. And don't worry — there isn't a bad seat in the house. Be sure to warm up your vocal cords before heading to the Tiki Room — the audience is asked to join in and "sing like the birdies sing." Very small kids may be a little spooked by a thunderstorm.

WHO AM I?

- I have antlers.
- I love carrots.
- Kristoff is my buddy.

Answer: Sven

Frontierland

Howdy, pardners! And welcome to the Wild West. Frontierland shows you what America was like when pioneers first settled west of the Mississippi River. It's also where you will find two of the best rides in the park. Both of them are special Disney mountains. You can take a watery trip down Splash Mountain and ride a runaway train at Big Thunder Mountain Railroad. These are just a few of the fun things to do here.

Tom Sawyer Island

There's only one way to get to Tom Sawyer Island — by raft. That's the way Tom himself used to travel. (Tom Sawyer is a character created by the author Mark Twain.)

Don't expect to find any rides here. In fact, compared to the rest of the Magic Kingdom, it is a pretty calm place. But if you bring your imagination, you can have exciting adventures of your own.

Bouncy bridges and secret exits

The island has a real windmill to wander through, hills to climb, and two bridges. One of them is an old barrel bridge. When one person bounces, everyone does. (Hold on to the ropes if you are worried about falling.)

Across one bridge is a big fort. An Audio-Animatronics blacksmith is working inside it. And there's a secret exit that is really a path through a dark and narrow cave.

In all, there are three caves to explore. They are the best things on the island. Beware: The caves are quite dark and may be a little scary.

Kids love it here

Tom Sawyer Island is fun for everyone. Most kids think the bridges and caves are the best part. Some folks like to bring snacks and have a picnic on the island. There are tables at a place called Aunt Polly's. From there, you can watch the Liberty Square Riverboat chug by.

READER REVIEW

I think every kid who comes to the Magic Kingdom should explore Tom Sawyer Island. I would have spent more time there if I could. The caves are the best part.

— Dan (age 12), Hummelstown, PA

PHOTO BY JILL SAFRO

FP+

Splash Mountain

#5 RIDE READER PLEASER

After riding Splash Mountain, you will know how it got its name. It's impossible to stay dry. There are three small dips leading up to a giant, splashy drop.

You're all wet

No matter which seat you sit in, there's a good chance you will get wet. But if you sit in the front, you are sure to get soaked. Don't worry, you'll dry off fast in the Florida sun.

The scenery tells the story

For now, you travel through scenes from a movie called *Song of the South*. In it, a character named Br'er Rabbit is trying to get away from Br'er Fox and Br'er Bear. When the rabbit goes over the edge toward the end, you go along for the ride. Try to keep your eyes open during the big drop — it won't be easy. Someday soon, this ride will have a new theme. It will be all about *The Princess and the Frog*!

READER REVIEW

Splash Mountain is one of my favorite rides because of the scenery. My favorite part is the big drop!

— Gregory (age 8), Canonsburg, PA

HOT TIP!

If you sit in the front or on the right side of the log, you get really wet!

HIDDEN MICKEY ALERT!

Look in the clouds during the final riverboat scene for a sleeping Mickey. (It comes after the big splash.)

WILD **SCARY** **WET**

YOU MUST BE AT LEAST 40 INCHES TALL TO RIDE SPLASH MOUNTAIN.

Big Thunder Mountain Railroad

Hang on to your hat and glasses, because this is one of the wildest rides in the wilderness. The speedy trains zip in, out, and over a huge, rocky mountain. They pass through scenes with real-looking chickens, goats, donkeys, and more.

The swoops and turns make this a thrilling roller coaster, but it's a bit tamer than Space Mountain. It's a ride you can go on again and again and see new things each time. Look for funny sights in the town — like the poor guy floating around in a bathtub. Try to ride during the day and again at night.

WILD **LOUD**

YOU MUST BE AT LEAST 40 INCHES TALL TO RIDE BIG THUNDER MOUNTAIN.

PHOTO BY JILL SAFRO

FP+

READER REVIEW

Big Thunder Mountain Railroad is a blast! I really like this attraction because it doesn't have a lot of dips. I think older kids would like it best — the hard turns might shock younger ones. What makes this ride seem very scary is the hard stop it comes to at the end.

— Taylor (age 11), Wyoming, MI

READER TIP

"During a parade is a good time to go to the most popular attractions — their lines may be shorter than usual."

— Joe (age 13), Roanoke, VA

Country Bear Jamboree

You have probably never seen bears quite like these. They sing songs, play instruments, and tell jokes. This is a silly show, so go in with a silly attitude. Big Al is one of the most popular bears. And he can't even carry a tune!

Everyone joins the show

Sometimes the audience sings and claps along with the performers. Even the furry heads on the wall join in on the fun. Melvin the moose, Buff the buffalo, and Buck the deer love to hang around the theater.

What do kids think of the bears?

The kooky country music show gets mixed reviews from kids. Some love it. Others aren't so thrilled. Younger kids seem to enjoy it the most. It's also a great place to cool off and rest up on a hot day.

Frontierland Shootin' Arcade

Yee-ha! This Western-themed arcade lets guests shoot beams of light at 100 different targets. For a dollar, you get 35 chances to hit targets in the town of Tombstone. There's a bank, a hotel, a jail, and a spooky cemetery. The arcade may not be open in all of 2022.

Liberty Square

What did America look like in Colonial days? Parts of it looked like Liberty Square. This small area separates Frontierland from Fantasyland. It's a quiet spot with some shops and a couple of popular attractions.

The Haunted Mansion

This haunted house isn't too scary, but there are plenty of ghosts to keep you on your toes. Before you enter, enjoy the interactive wait area and read the funny tombstones outside. (We like the one that says: HERE LIES GOOD OLD FRED. A GREAT BIG ROCK FELL ON HIS HEAD.)

Once inside, you'll be in a room with no windows and no doors. At first, it seems as if there's no way out. It is spooky!

There's a moment before you board a "Doom Buggy" when the room is totally dark. It's just a few seconds, but for some, it's much too long.

The Doom Buggy doesn't move very quickly, but it is still hard to catch all the eerie details. Watch for the door knockers that knock all by themselves, a ghostly teapot pouring tea, and a ghost napping under the table at a party in the ballroom.

READER REVIEW

The Haunted Mansion is spooky at first, but then it is loads of fun. My favorite scene is the waltzing ghosts. Older kids will enjoy this attraction. Younger kids might find this scary. I think it's a very cool ride.

— Will (age 12), Greenville, SC

#9 RIDE ★ READER PLEASER ★

DARK

SCARY

FP+

The Hall of Presidents

The first part of this attraction is a film about U.S. history. Then the screen rises and all of the American presidents are on stage together. They are robots called Audio-Animatronics, but they look real. If you watch closely, you will notice the presidents move, nod, and blink.

The attraction is in a building that looks like Independence Hall. (The real Independence Hall is in the city of Philadelphia, Pennsylvania.) Each show is about 22 minutes long. Some details will change in 2022.

Liberty Square Riverboat

The *Liberty Belle* riverboat docks in Liberty Square. This big steamboat takes guests on slow, relaxing cruises. It can be a nice break on a busy day (though there aren't many seats). The best spots are right up front or in the back, where you can see both sides of the river as you float along. The 47-foot-tall boat uses steam power. The steam turns the paddle wheel, which makes the boat move. Pretty cool!

Fantasyland

Fantasyland is home to many magical rides that younger kids love. Older kids and even grown-ups enjoy them, too. These attractions are popular, and the waits can be quite long. But the lines are sometimes shorter while people watch a parade or a fireworks show. It's a good idea to skip the parade one day and spend time in Fantasyland. The land may be less crowded late in the day, too.

Prince Charming Regal Carrousel

Most of the attractions at Walt Disney World were dreamed up by Disney Imagineers. But not this carrousel. It was discovered in New Jersey, where it was once part of another amusement park. It was built around 1917.

When you climb on a horse for your ride on the carrousel, be sure to notice that each horse is different. And remember to look up at the ceiling and its hand-painted scenes from *Cinderella*. While you ride, listen for famous Disney tunes, including "When You Wish Upon a Star" and "Be Our Guest."

The Barnstormer

One of the wildest rides in Fantasyland is a roller coaster in Storybook Circus. This ride may look small, but it packs plenty of thrills. It takes you on a twisting and turning flight high above the park.

The trip starts out slow, but watch out! Before you know it, you will be soaring through the circus. Hang on tight.

Before you board, be sure to check out the magical area surrounding the ride — that Goofy really is quite goofy.

WILD   SCARY

YOU MUST BE 35 INCHES TALL TO RIDE THE BARNSTORMER.

FP+

FP+

Mad Tea Party

The idea for the giant teacups that spin through this ride came from a scene in *Alice in Wonderland*. In the story, the Mad Hatter throws himself a tea party to celebrate his un-birthday. That's any day of the year that is not his birthday!

At the Mad Tea Party, you control how fast your cup spins by turning the big wheel in the center. The more you turn, the more you spin. Or you can just sit back and let the cup spin on its own. It may be hard while you are whirling, but try to take a peek at the little mouse that keeps popping out of the big teapot in the center. He is super cute.

WILD

Dumbo the Flying Elephant

Just like the star of the movie *Dumbo*, these elephants know how to fly. They would love to take you for a short ride (about two minutes) above Fantasyland. A button lets you control the up-and-down movement of the elephant.

Take your kid brother or sister

Many kids agree that this ride is super fun for younger kids. But they all find something to like and think it would be fun to go on with a little brother or sister.

Beware of long lines

Even though Dumbo has doubled in size (so more people can ride), the line for this ride tends to be long. Get a Fastpass if you can. If not, you can play in a circus-themed play area while you wait. (A text will let your parents know when it is your time to ride.) If the wait is too long when you get there, try again toward the end of the day. That's when many young kids have already gone home.

READER REVIEW

I think this ride is more fun if you go on it with your little brother or sister. I like that you can control how high or low you want to be.

— Rachel (age 10),
Franklin, TN

HOT TIP!

Need to cool off? Or do you just enjoy jumping in puddles? Head to the Casey Junior Splash and Soak Station. You'll be glad you did!

PHOTO BY JILL SAFRO

#16 RIDE
READER PLEASER

FP+

PHOTO BY JILL SAFRO

 HOT TIP!

Would you like to meet Disney princesses? Head to Princess Fairytale Hall. Royal folks such as Cinderella and Rapunzel greet guests throughout the day. They may meet you inside, or from a distance just outside the hall.

Peter Pan's Flight

Swoop and soar through scenes that tell the story of how Wendy, Michael, and John get sprinkled with pixie dust and fly off to Never Land with Peter Pan and Tinker Bell. Along the way, you see Princess Tiger Lily, Captain Hook, and Hook's sidekick, Mr. Smee.

Near the beginning of the trip, there's a beautiful scene of London at night. Notice that the cars on the streets really move. Later, watch out for the crocodile that wants to munch on Captain Hook.

When you first board your pirate ship, it seems like you are riding on a track on the ground. Once you get going, the track is above you, so it feels like the ship is really flying.

#13 RIDE
READER PLEASER

DARK

It's a Small World

People have a lot in common, no matter where they live. That's the point of this attraction. In it, you take a slow boat ride through several large rooms where singing dolls represent different parts of the world. There are Greek dancers, Japanese kite flyers, Scottish bagpipers, and many more. There's also a jungle scene with hippos, giraffes, and monkeys.

All the colorful scenery is set to the song "It's a Small World, After All." The signs at the end say goodbye in different languages. *Aloha! Shalom! Sayonara! Adios!*

#14 RIDE READER PLEASER

PHOTO BY JILL SAFRO

HIDDEN MICKEY ALERT!

Many Mickeys can be found in the vines you see in the African scene of It's a Small World.

FP+

FP+

The Many Adventures of Winnie the Pooh

Winnie the Pooh loves his honey. In fact, he will do anything to keep the sweet treat safe. On this trip through the Hundred Acre Wood, see what Pooh must do to rescue his honey pots and his friends, too.

The blustery day

The wind is howling, the leaves are rustling, and everything in Pooh's world is blowing away. Roo and Piglet are up in the air. And Owl's house is about to topple over. Hold on tight, or you just might be swept away next! (Not really.)

A sticky situation

Finally the wind calms and Pooh can get to sleep. But when he wakes up from his silly dream, it's raining. Pooh's honey pots are about to wash away in the flood. He can save them, but will he save himself?

This attraction has an interactive wait area. Some kids think it's almost as much fun as the attraction itself. Be sure to check it out!

Seven Dwarfs Mine Train

Are you ready to visit the mine where a million diamonds shine? Then head to Seven Dwarfs Mine Train! The popular attraction is a roller coaster with a twist — the cars move up and down along the track and they sway a bit from side to side!

Heigh ho, heigh ho!

If you have seen *Snow White and the Seven Dwarfs*, you know where Sleepy, Dopey, Doc, and their friends work — in a diamond mine. At this attraction, guests board train cars and see that colorful mine.

Hang on tight

It's not as speedy as Space Mountain, or as rough as the big drop in Splash Mountain, but this ride can spook some kids. If the Barnstormer is too scary for you, skip this coaster.

READER REVIEW

If you are looking for a fun ride, stop here! I love the sharp turns and the big drop. Make sure to see the dwarfs and the gems in the mine. I think this is a great ride for people of all ages. You should go at least twice!

— Gianna (age 10), Au Gres, MI

FP+

WILD · SCARY · DARK

YOU MUST BE AT LEAST 38 INCHES TALL TO RIDE SEVEN DWARFS MINE TRAIN.

FP+

Under the Sea — Journey of The Little Mermaid

This attraction invites you to join Ariel for an adventure. Are you ready to dive in? You will go "under the sea" by boarding a special vehicle called a clam-mobile. (They are giant shells, like the ones over at The Seas with Nemo and Friends in EPCOT.) And don't worry about getting wet — the water here is just a cool special effect.

Once you board your clam-mobile, the journey begins. Along the way, you will meet up with Ariel, Flounder, and all of their pals. There is a lot to see and hear in this attraction — you may have to ride it twice to take it all in!

Mickey's PhilharMagic FP+

It's magical. It's musical. It's three-dimensional. It's Mickey's PhilharMagic.

Donald Duck is the real star of this 3-D movie, but it's not a one-duck show. He is joined by his friends Ariel, Aladdin, Jasmine, Simba, and, of course, Mickey Mouse.

A one and a two and a three-D

The show takes place in a grand concert hall. Once guests (that's you!) find seats and put on 3-D glasses, it's showtime.

Sit back, relax, and enjoy as the cast of characters show off their musical talents. (Some are more talented than others.) And be sure to keep your eyes and ears open — a whole lot happens at the same time.

Eye-popping 3-D effects take place on the oversize movie screen. Music fills the air. And special surprises happen inside the theater.

What's a PhilharMagic?

In case you were wondering . . . Disney Imagineers made up the word PhilharMagic. They based it on the real word *philharmonic*, which describes a group of musicians who play their instruments at the same time.

LOUD   DARK

Enchanted Tales with Belle

Would you like to help Belle tell "the tale as old as time" — the story of *Beauty and the Beast*? You are invited to her dad's cottage to do just that. The fun starts by taking a step through a magical mirror. It transports guests all the way to Beast's castle. There you will meet Madame Wardrobe and her assistant. Together they assign roles to audience members — wave your hand when they ask for volunteers. Once the roles are assigned, guests walk to the library. Expect to be greeted by Lumiere, the candlestick from *Beauty and the Beast*. When Belle arrives, it is story time. This is a popular attraction and the long line moves slowly. Get a Fastpass if it is offered. FP+

Tomorrowland

Tomorrowland began as a view of the future. As the real world changed, so did this land. Now it's like a city from a science fiction story. The palm trees are made of metal. The rides here let you rocket through space or zoom through the sky. And a famous Space Ranger pops in to visit with guests. A good way to see this land is to ride on the Tomorrowland Transit Authority PeopleMover — it's a relaxing tour and a nice rest for your feet. And even though you won't have a driver's license until the future, you can drive a car in Tomorrowland right now — as long as you are tall enough.

READER REVIEW

I love the thrill of riding through Tomorrowland and going through attractions. The turns can be a bit bumpy, but the PeopleMover is mostly relaxing. My dad and I love to look for Hidden Mickeys.

— Sydney (age 10),
Leland, NC

DARK

Tomorrowland Transit Authority PeopleMover

This slow-moving ride travels by or through many Tomorrowland attractions. You will even get a peek at Buzz Lightyear's Space Ranger Spin. Pay attention, because you pass by the window very quickly. You will also go through Space Mountain, but you won't see much because it's totally dark.

This ride is a good one to head to when it's hot out. The cars move just fast enough to make a nice breeze. It's interesting to know that the ride doesn't make any pollution. And the wait is usually very short. Everybody loves that!

FP+

Space Mountain

Thrill seekers head straight for this rocket ride through outer space. It has twists, turns, and a few steep dips. And it all takes place in the dark! Space Mountain is one of the most popular rides in Walt Disney World.

Who turned out the lights?

It's so dark inside Space Mountain that you barely see where you are going. It gets scary — especially if you sit in the front of the rocket. The darkness makes the ride exciting. Every curve comes as a surprise.

You will hear sounds of other rockets zooming around. Of course, the coaster is perfectly safe. The noises are meant to add to the excitement.

Is it too scary?

There's no doubt about it: Space Mountain is scary. But some kids say it's a "good scary." The rockets travel about 28 miles per hour, but it feels much faster.

WILD   SCARY   DARK

YOU MUST BE AT LEAST 44 INCHES TALL TO RIDE SPACE MOUNTAIN.

Walt Disney's Carousel of Progress

A lot has changed since the year 1900. Most homes had no electricity, water came from a well, nobody had a TV, and mobile phones didn't exist. Life was rough! This attraction shows how American family life has changed since then.

A moving experience

The show is really four short plays. And the performers are all Audio-Animatronics actors. After each scene, the theater moves to the right. That's when you will hear the song "There's a Great, Big, Beautiful Tomorrow." Feel free to sing along.

Walt made it special

Some kids find the show a bit on the slow side, but others think it's quite special. Why? It was introduced to the world by Walt Disney himself. The special event didn't happen at Disney World (it wasn't open yet), but at the World's Fair in New York City in 1964. The attraction has been updated, but the show is still an amusing look at American life. And the Carousel of Progress has made history, too — it has had more performances than any other stage show in the history of American theater.

READER REVIEW

This is a classic show that should not be missed. I recommend this attraction for kids who are interested in history. It teaches about American life from the 1900s to the 1990s.

— Nicole (age 12), Sunburst, MT

FP+

Monsters, Inc. Laugh Floor

Buzz Lightyear has funny neighbors in Tomorrowland Mike, Roz, and other characters from the movie *Monsters, Inc.* They are all part of a silly attraction that lets you interact with your animated friends. That's right, the audience members not only watch the show — they are a part of it. Don't worry. The monsters don't want to make kids scream the way they did in the movie. This time, they want to make kids laugh. So be ready for lots of wackiness and some very silly jokes!

This show may not be open in all of 2022.

#12 RIDE
★ READER PLEASER ★

Buzz Lightyear's Space Ranger Spin

In this attraction, everyone is the size of a toy — including you. In fact, you are so small, you fit inside a video game shooting gallery.

To infinity and beyond!

The ride is under the command of Buzz Lightyear. You've just become a Junior Space Ranger, so you are under his command, too. Together, you battle the evil Emperor Zurg.

Zap that Zurg

Zurg and his robots are stealing batteries from other toys. They plan to use the batteries to power their ultimate weapon of destruction. Your job is to fight back. Use the laser cannons in your spaceship to aim at the targets (they look like Z's) and zap Zurg's power. Every time you hit a target, you earn more points. There is a scoreboard next to the laser cannon. It keeps track of all the points you earn.

At the end of the ride, you'll pass a chart. It shows everyone's ranger rank based on their score. Check to see where your score falls. Most kids improve with practice.

Astro Orbiter

In the middle of Tomorrowland, there is a giant, glowing tower. It is called Rocket Tower. The Astro Orbiter ride is all the way at the top. In it, you soar past colorful planets high above Tomorrowland.

Like on Dumbo the Flying Elephant, you control how high or low your rocket flies. You can ride by yourself or with a friend. (Each rocket fits two people.) But if you want to be the one to control how high you go, be sure to sit in the front.

FP+

TRON Lightcycle/Run

A powerful new attraction is racing into the Magic Kingdom — TRON Lightcycle/Run. In it, riders zip through a tunnel of flashing lights and zoom along a turbo-charged track. Exciting music and 3-D graphics make this roller coaster very special. And wow is it fast. In fact, it's one of the fastest indoor coasters ever built in a Disney park.

TRON Lightcycle/Run is expected to open in 2022. It should be a big a hit with daredevils. But it may be too intense for some kids. Do not eat or drink just before you ride.

LOUD   DARK   SCARY

YOU MUST BE AT LEAST 48 INCHES TALL TO RIDE TRON LIGHTCYCLE/RUN.

#15 RIDE
★ READER PLEASER ★

TOMORROWLAND
SPEEDWAY

FP+

READER REVIEW

I love this ride. No matter what your age (if you are tall enough), you can drive your parents for once! The race track is nice and long. The line to ride is long, too — but it's worth the wait.

— Lauren (age 12),
Harrisburg, PA

READER TIP

"If you get lost at Walt Disney World, don't worry. Just go to the nearest Cast Member (a worker wearing a name tag) and ask for help."

— Sam (age 9),
Eatontown, NJ

Tomorrowland Speedway

You don't need a license to drive around this racetrack (as long as you are at least 32 inches tall and riding with someone at least 54 inches tall). The race cars travel along a rail, but it's not as easy as it looks. Even experts bounce around a bit — and laugh a lot. The race cars are real and are powered by gasoline.

There is something strange about these cars. They don't have any brakes! Just take your foot off the gas pedal and the car comes to a stop.

If you are at least 54 inches tall, you can drive by yourself. If you are between 32 and 54 inches, you're allowed to steer the car — as long as your passenger is at least 54 inches tall. Your passenger can press the gas pedal for you. Don't forget to fasten your seatbelt!

Entertainment

The Magic Kingdom is a very entertaining place. It seems like there is always a show starting or a parade going by. Read on to learn about some events that have happened in the park. Which shows will go on during your visit? Ask a parent to visit *disneyworld.com* to find out. Expect lots of surprises, too. Walt Disney World is celebrating 50 years of magic!

Festival of Fantasy Parade

Disney characters star in this afternoon parade. You might even get to meet characters as they pass by. Say hi to Anna and Elsa on the *Frozen* float! And don't miss the giant fire-breathing dragon. It's super cool. Line up early to get a spot on the curb.

This parade usually runs in the afternoon. It may be replaced with a new parade in 2022.

Once Upon a Time

Cinderella Castle becomes a giant movie screen during this 14-minute show. In it, Chip asks Mrs. Potts to tell him a story. She is happy to share tales from *Cinderella*, *Winnie the Pooh*, *Peter Pan*, *Tangled*, and more.

This show happens just before or right after Happily Ever After (fireworks show). Details may change in 2022.

Let the Magic Begin!

The Magic Kingdom park welcomes guests with a special show each morning. The fun begins with all guests being called to the area by Cinderella Castle. Soon Mickey Mouse and his friends come to the stage to welcome you to the park in true Disney fashion. Let the magic begin!

Casey's Corner Piano

If you visit Main Street during the day, you may hear tunes being played on a piano. Some are Disney songs and others are old-fashioned ones that your parents will know. They'll all make you tap your toes. You'll find the piano player by Casey's Corner restaurant on Main Street, U.S.A.

Citizens of Main Street

Do you know what a citizen is? The word describes a person who lives in a particular town or city. You are a citizen of your town or city. And the folks who call the Magic Kingdom home are called Citizens of Main Street. They are actually performers — and they're there to entertain guests like you. Look for friendly folks dressed like they lived a long time ago. There's a firefighter, baseball player, and others. They are all happy to chat and pose for photos.

Happy 50th Anniversary, Walt Disney World!

Something very special happened in Florida on October 1, 1971. Walt Disney World welcomed its first guests! Back then, there was just one theme park. Can you guess which one? If you said Magic Kingdom, you are right.

All of Walt Disney World is marking its 50th anniversary — and the Magic Kingdom has a lot to celebrate. At the center of it all is Cinderella Castle. And it seems like it has been sprinkled with pixie dust! Be sure to see it at night — that's when the castle really shines.

The 50th anniversary celebration will last more than a year. That's some party! To learn more about 50th anniversary shows and activities, ask a parent to visit *disneyworld.com*. (They can also use the My Disney Experience app or website.)

The Main Street Trolley Show

If you visit the Magic Kingdom before lunch time, you may catch this old-fashioned musical show. In it, performers arrive on a very jolly trolley and break into song and dance. You just might find yourself singing or humming along — especially to "Walkin' Right Down the Middle of Main Street, U.S.A." It's a catchy tune!

Dapper Dans

The Dapper Dans are a four-person singing group known as a Barbershop Quartet. They entertain guests on Main Street, U.S.A. during the day. Stop in for a show at the barbershop or out on Main Street. They may even perform from their bicycle built for four. That's talent!

Main Street Philharmonic

A marching band makes merry music on Main Street, U.S.A. The band members wear bright red-and-white uniforms, so they are easy to spot. But there is an easier way to find them: Follow your ears!

Mickey's Royal Friendship Faire

Mickey and his pals like to celebrate their friendship with song and dance — and they want you to join them. This musical show takes place in front of Cinderella Castle on most days. In it, Disney friends perform to music from *The Princess and the Frog, Frozen, Tangled*, and other films.

The fun includes appearances by lots of Disney characters — Goofy, Donald, Daisy, Tiana, Prince Naveen, Rapunzel, Flynn Rider, Anna, Elsa, Olaf, Minnie, and Mickey.

Mickey's Royal Friendship Faire takes place on an outdoor stage. It may be canceled if the weather is bad at showtime.

A new show might replace Mickey's Royal Friendship Faire in 2022.

Happily Ever After

There is a happy ending to every day at the Magic Kingdom! This colorful fireworks show takes place high in the sky — up above and all around Cinderella Castle. It captures the heart, humor, and heroism of Disney storytelling.

The show also includes animated projections, laser lights, and merry music. It lasts for about 18 minutes. Don't worry if you can't find space to watch on Main Street — the fireworks can be seen from lots of spots around the park.

READER REVIEW

I love this amazing fireworks show. The special effects make it seem like the characters are right on the castle! Do not miss this "only at Walt Disney World" experience!

— Sarah (age 11), Pinckney, MI

The Muppets Present . . . Great Moments in American History

The Muppets' take on American history is a little wacky — but it is also quite entertaining. See for yourself at this funny outdoor show in Liberty Square. It happens in the windows around the Hall of Presidents attraction. This show is only presented during very busy times of year — usually during holiday seasons. Will the show happen during your visit? Ask a parent to visit *disneyworld.com* to find out.

Where to Find Characters
at the Magic Kingdom

Disney characters love to greet park guests. In 2021, they all did so from a safe distance—from parade floats, spots behind fancy ropes, and more. That may continue in 2022. But they may also greet guests in other ways. Mickey Mouse may greet folks at Main Street's **Town Square Theater**. Tinker Bell could be there, too. Lots of different characters show up on Main Street throughout the day.

Looking to meet Disney princesses? Go to **Princess Fairytale Hall** in Fantasyland. Minnie Mouse, Daisy Duck, Goofy, and Donald hang out at **Pete's Silly Sideshow** in the

Storybook Circus part of Fantasyland. Elsewhere in Fantasyland you may see Alice and her friends from Wonderland, plus Peter Pan, Gaston (near his Tavern), Ariel (in her grotto), Winnie the Pooh, Tigger, and others. Aladdin and Jasmine may appear in **Adventureland**.

When you're in Tomorrowland, keep an eye out for Stitch and Buzz Lightyear. Merida from *Brave* may stop by the **Fairytale Garden** (an area next to Cinderella Castle).

Another way to see favorite Disney pals is at parades and stage shows. You may even get to dance with some of them.

TIPS

 Head to this theme park first, since it has the most rides for kids.

Try to arrive just before the park opens and watch Let the Magic Begin. It's a character-filled show at Cinderella Castle. (It may not be offered during all of 2022.)

You may have a chance to meet Mickey Mouse in Main Street's Town Square Theater. Use page 150 of this book for his autograph. Bring a camera, too!

Want a break from long lines? These attractions usually have short waits: The PeopleMover, Country Bear Jamboree, The Enchanted Tiki Room, Carousel of Progress, and The Hall of Presidents.

Need to cool off on a hot day? Get wet at Casey Junior Splash and Soak Station in Fantasyland. Or hop on the PeopleMover and enjoy the breeze.

If the Magic Kingdom is open late, it's fun to go on your favorite outdoor attractions after dark.

There are "chicken exits" in the lines for all scary rides, just in case you change your mind about riding at the last minute.

Do not eat just before riding Astro Orbiter, TRON Lightcycle/Run, The Barnstormer, Space Mountain, Seven Dwarfs Mine Train, the Mad Tea Party, or Big Thunder Mountain Railroad.

If you have never been on a roller coaster, ride The Barnstormer first. If you enjoy it, try Seven Dwarfs Mine Train next — but remember, it is scarier!

 Ask characters to sign pages 150 to 157 of this book. If they aren't signing autographs during your visit, they can pose in the backround of a selfie!

Attraction Ratings

VERY COOL
(Don't miss!)

- Astro Orbiter
- Mad Tea Party
- Jungle Cruise
- Mickey's PhilharMagic
- Dumbo the Flying Elephant
- Enchanted Tales with Belle
- The Magic Carpets of Aladdin
- The Many Adventures of Winnie the Pooh
- Tom Sawyer Island
- The Barnstormer
- Under the Sea — Journey of The Little Mermaid
- Tomorrowland Transit Authority PeopleMover

COOL
(Check it out!)

- Country Bear Jamboree
- Monsters, Inc. Laugh Floor
- Prince Charming Regal Carrousel
- Swiss Family Treehouse
- Liberty Square Riverboat
- Walt Disney's Enchanted Tiki Room
- Walt Disney's Carousel of Progress
- Walt Disney World Railroad
- The Hall of Presidents

COOLEST
(See at least twice!)

- Splash Mountain
- Big Thunder Mountain Railroad
- The Haunted Mansion
- Peter Pan's Flight
- Buzz Lightyear's Space Ranger Spin
- Pirates of the Caribbean
- Space Mountain
- It's a Small World
- Seven Dwarfs Mine Train
- Tomorrowland Speedway
- TRON Lightcycle/Run

WHAT DO YOU THINK?

The kids who helped with this book rated all the attractions at Walt Disney World. But your opinion counts, too! If you would like to vote on your favorite attractions, send us an email and we'll send you a survey form. Be sure to get a parent's permission first. We'll use your survey when we create next year's book. (Our email address is on page 7.)

Where's Mickey?

Disney Imagineers have hidden Mickey Mouse's image all over the Magic Kingdom. Here are a few places to search for Hidden Mickeys while you are in the park. Would you like to see Mickey in person? Visit City Hall on Main Street — the Cast Members will know where he is.

The Haunted Mansion

In the ghost party room, check out the bottom of the banquet table. There is a Hidden Mickey made out of saucers and a plate. (It's on the left side of the table.)

Carousel of Progress

There are a few Hidden Mickeys in the attraction's Christmas scene. Our favorite is the one on top of the fireplace. It is a Mickey nutcracker! Can you find others?

Tomorrowland Transit Authority PeopleMover

After gliding past the Metro Retro Society, look to the right. There you'll see a lady getting her hair done. What's on her belt? A Hidden Mickey!

Buzz Lightyear's Space Ranger Spin

Once you enter the Buzz building, look for a poster on the right and find the planet called Pollost Prime. One of the continents on the map forms Mickey's profile. And keep your eyes open during the space video scene (about halfway through the ride). You will see this same planet fly by on the right.

It's a Small World

During the ride, pay close attention in the Africa room. If you search the purple leaves on the ceiling, you may spot several Hidden Mickeys. (They are close to the giraffes.)

EPCOT

EPCOT is a great place to make discoveries about the world. At this park, things that used to seem ordinary suddenly become fun. Most of the attractions at EPCOT are in buildings called pavilions (pronounced: *puh-VILL-yuhnz*). The pavilions are in four areas of the park — World Celebration, World Nature, World Discovery, and World Showcase. EPCOT's neighborhoods celebrate inventions, ideas, and the wonders of nature. The areas explore everything — from the food we eat and your family car to the land, sea, and outer space. (Some details may change in 2022.)

World Showcase lets you travel around the world without leaving the park! There are many different countries to visit here. Each country has copies of its famous buildings, restaurants, and other landmarks. Together, they will make you feel as if you are visiting the real place.

WORLD SHOWCASE

WORLD SHOWCASE
LAGOON

N

WORLD DISCOVERY

WORLD CELEBRATION

ENTRANCE PLAZA

WORLD NATURE

TO BUSES

INTERNATIONAL GATEWAY

DISNEY SKYLINER

WORLD CELEBRATION

1 Spaceship Earth
2 Imagination!

WORLD NATURE

3 The Seas
4 The Land

WORLD DISCOVERY

5 Test Track
6 Mission: SPACE
7 PLAY! Pavilion
8 Guardians of the Galaxy:
  Cosmic Rewind

WORLD SHOWCASE

9 Showcase Plaza
10 Mexico
11 Norway
12 China
13 Germany
14 Italy
15 The American Adventure

16 Japan
17 Morocco
18 France
19 United Kingdom
20 Canada

Use this map to explore EPCOT.

World Celebration

When you enter EPCOT by monorail, you are in the area called World Celebration. It shows how we connect to each other and to the world around us. The big attraction here is called Spaceship Earth.

Spaceship Earth FP+

You can't miss the silver ball that is the symbol of EPCOT. It's gigantic! The Spaceship Earth ride is inside the big, round building. (The structure is called a geosphere.) The attraction has been around since EPCOT opened in 1982. But the show inside has changed over the years. In fact, it may change again in 2022! The story explores human achievements from many years ago up until today. Many folks call Spaceship Earth the Big Golf Ball. Can you guess why?

After the ride, you can spend some time in the "Project Tomorrow" area. It's filled with interactive exhibits.

This pavilion may not be open in all of 2022.

READER REVIEW

Some people think this ride is not worth a long wait, but it's one of my family's favorites. It may be a calm ride, but I think it's very interesting. It's a classic!

— Amy (age 12), Clinton, NJ

READER TIP

"The line for Spaceship Earth is usually shortest toward the end of the day!"

— Kersie (age 12), Vancouver, WA

DREAMER'S POINT

Walt Disney was a dreamer. And he worked hard to make his dreams come true. One of his dreams was to build a place for grown-ups and kids to have fun together. That dream became Walt Disney World.

Imagineers are building a place for you to dream like Walt. It is a garden called Dreamer's Point. When it opens, it will be filled with plant life and a special statue of Walt Disney. There will be a spot to make wishes, too. The Wishing Tree grows in a part of the garden called the Enchanted Forest. Another place to visit is called Story Fountain. It celebrates the power and music of Disney storytelling.

Do you have dreams and wishes? Dreamer's Point is a great spot to think about making them come true.

IMAGINATION!

This place is a workout for your imagination — the attractions really make you think. There is a ride that tests your creativity and an activity center. Outside, the jumping waters of the Leap Frog Fountains are sure to cool you off. There are a lot of other ways to have fun here, too. Just use your imagination!

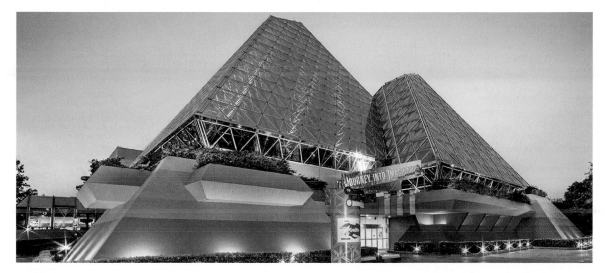

Disney and Pixar Short Film Festival FP+

The Magic Eye Theater is a bit unusual — its shows are in 4-D. The films are in 3-D and the theater has special "4-D" effects. Before the action starts, guests watch a pre-show video. In it, Disney and Pixar artists explain how they create animation. As you enter the theater, pick up 3-D glasses. Put them on once you're safely settled in your seat. The first of three short films is called *Get a Horse*. It's a wacky wagon-ride adventure starring Minnie, Mickey, and the rest of the gang. The other movies change from time to time, but they are sure to put a smile on your face. This is a nice place to escape the heat and enjoy animated films. Details may change in 2022.

HOT TIP!

See the attractions inside the Imagination pavilion BEFORE you splash at the Leap Frog Fountains. Otherwise you will be super soggy as you sit through the shows.

Journey Into Imagination with Figment

Think about how different the world would be without imagination in it. There would be no stories to tell, no pictures to draw, and no inventions to make things easier. One thing is for sure — Walt Disney World would not exist!

Imagination is so important to the folks at Disney that they made a special place in EPCOT to learn all about it. It is called the Imagination Institute — and it is having an open house. That means everyone is invited to learn about its projects. And who better to take you on a tour of this special place than Figment himself? (Figment is a little purple dragon. He hosts this attraction. That's him in the picture. A lot of kids are Figment fans.)

As you exit the attraction, check out the Imageworks play area. It has a few hands-on and feet-on activities. Imageworks may not be open in all of 2022.

LEAP FROG FOUNTAINS

There are lots of places to jump over water at Walt Disney World — hotel pools, lazy rivers at the water parks, and theme park spray zones. But there is a special place where water jumps over you. EPCOT is home to the famous Leap Frog Fountains. Stop by to watch streams of water leap through the air, land with a little splash, then soar again. Kids love to stand under the flying streams of water. Some kids try to catch them! The jumping water is a popular spot for folks to cool off when the weather is warm. You'll find these fountains by the Imagination pavilion.

DID YOU KNOW?

Figment made his first EPCOT appearance in 1983. Where did he come from? The dragon was made by a wizard called Dreamfinder. He collected many interesting items from around the world — tiny wings, yellow eyes, the snout of a crocodile, childish delight, a bit of purple pigment, and more. When he put it all together, he created Figment. Thanks, Dreamfinder!

World Discovery

PLAY! Pavilion

A whole new experience is coming to EPCOT — and it's not like anything else at the park. It's all about the power of play. Everything inside involves fun. It is a bit like a small city in a big building. And the city is bursting with interactive games, hands-on activities, entertainment, and Disney character experiences. Have you seen the movie *Ralph Breaks the Internet*? The inside of this building may remind you of that film. It's a colorful playground. And it is fun for guests of all ages — as long as they love to play.

The EPCOT Play pavilion is expected to open by the end of 2022. Details may change. To learn more about it, check out *disneyworld.com* (with a parent).

WHO AM I?

- I'm a rodent.
- Nuts are my go-to snack.
- I have a red nose.

Answer: Dale

DARK

WILD

LOUD

Guardians of the Galaxy: Cosmic Rewind

You can zoom through space with Groot, Rocket the Raccoon, and other pals at this thrilling new attraction. Guardians of the Galaxy: Cosmic Rewind is an indoor roller coaster. It's a very wild ride, but not too scary for daredevils. The experience is different from most roller coasters in one way: the ride vehicles rotate (move in a circle) as they zip along the track. It is very exciting!

If the idea of speeding through dark space on a roller coaster sounds too spooky, you should skip this ride. And please don't eat just before you go.

Guardians of the Galaxy: Cosmic Rewind is expected to open in 2022. Are you tall enough to ride? Ask a parent to check *disneyworld.com* to find out.

DID YOU KNOW?

EPCOT's International Flower and Garden Festival takes place each spring. It's a colorful celebration of Earth's natural beauty — especially its plants and flowers. It would take you a very long time to stop and smell each one. There are more than 30 million blossoms in all.

WHO AM I?

- My last name is Bjorgman.
- I spend a lot of time around ice.
- I think reindeer are better than people.

Answer: Kristoff

Mission: SPACE

Three . . . two . . . one . . . blast-off! This ride lets you know what it's like to be an astronaut on a trip to outer space. Here, you can take a rocket to Mars or enjoy a trip around Earth.

The Mars voyage is the Orange Mission. It is intense. The orbit around our planet is calmer. It's called the Green Mission.

Each spacecraft holds four guests. Once aboard, it's time for take-off. You will feel the tug of gravity during the Orange Mission launch — just like on a NASA spacecraft. This part lasts nearly a minute, so be ready.

What's your job?

Once you're on your way, things calm down a bit. That may be when you realize you have a job to do. Are you the commander, engineer, pilot, or navigator? That depends on where you sit. It doesn't matter — all the jobs are fun to do. Just before the Orange Mission ends, you will get a strange sensation. It's not weightlessness, but it is definitely out of this world. It's a lot like the feeling astronauts get in outer space.

Mission accomplished

If bouncing or spinning makes you sick, skip the Orange Mission — a lot of people get quite woozy on it. Some feel sick afterward. You can take a cool trip around the Earth, instead — just ask for the Green Mission. Be sure to check the Advanced Training Lab near the Mission SPACE exit. It has activities that most kids enjoy. The lab may not be open in all of 2022.

LOUD

WILD

DARK

YOU MUST BE AT LEAST 40 INCHES TALL TO RIDE MISSION SPACE.

FP+

CAPABILITY

EFFICIENCY

#7 RIDE
READER PLEASER

READER REVIEW

I was four years old the first time I rode Test Track and I screamed like I never had before! As soon as it was over, I begged to go back on. It was so much fun. It's very fast and thrilling. A great ride.

— Brylee (age 12), McCormick, SC

HOT TIP!

Put long hair in a ponytail before riding Test Track, or it might get all tangled up. And hold onto your hat!

DID YOU KNOW?

The track in Test Track is nearly a mile long. That makes it one of the longest tracks at any Walt Disney World attraction.

Test Track

What is it like to create and test a car? You can find out at this attraction — and learn what it's like to make a new car that is as safe as can be.

Where are the brakes?

Test Track is one of Walt Disney World's fastest rides and EPCOT's original thrill ride. After you design a car on a touch screen, you can test it on the track. As you enter your car, you may notice it does not have brakes or a working steering wheel. Don't worry. It is a self-driving car! And its sound and video equipment let you know what's being tested. You zip around curves, zoom down a street, and reach a speed of 65 miles per hour. At one point, your car nearly crashes into a truck!

A crash course in car design

Kids think this ride is a fun way to learn about cars. Parts of it are loud, so don't be startled if you hear a noisy crash. And remember — the ride is safe. Disney workers tested all the cars. After all, that's what test-driving is all about. After the ride, check out the post-show area. It's pretty cool.

WILD

LOUD

SCARY

DARK

YOU MUST BE AT LEAST 40 INCHES TALL TO RIDE.

World Nature

READER REVIEW

My family and I spent hours at this pavilion. The ride is superb and it is home to thousands of gorgeous fish. Be sure to check out the manatees. They're adorable!

— Lauren (age 14), Deerfield Beach, FL

The Seas

It's easy to find Nemo these days — he is in a building called The Seas with Nemo and Friends! He and his pals can't wait for you to visit. There are more than 2,000 real sea creatures here. There is also a ride, a shark-themed area, and sea-based exhibits to explore.

After taking a quick look at the aquarium, you will enter an area called Sea Base. This is your chance to take a closer look at the creatures and to try out the hands-on exhibits. Be sure to visit the Nemo and Friends room, where you can find a real-life version of the little guy. Many kids get a kick out of Bruce's Shark World. (It's a play area where you can learn about sharks.)

The Seas with Nemo & Friends FP+

Jump inside a clam-mobile and let the adventure begin. It's a class trip run by Nemo's teacher, Mr. Ray. It seems little Nemo has wandered off again. Your job is to help find him. Expect to see Dory, Bruce, Chum, Crush, Squirt, and others along the way. And don't worry about Nemo — he won't stay lost for long.

The slow-moving trip under the sea lasts about 6 minutes.

DARK

Turtle Talk with Crush FP+

Everyone seems to love Turtle Talk with Crush. It is a show that lets you talk to the 150-year-old cartoon critter. The best part? He talks back.

The show takes place in a small theater. Grown-ups like to sit on the benches, but most kids prefer the floor in front of the big screen. From the moment Crush swims onto the screen, he has everyone laughing. He asks questions, tells jokes, and make comments about the different "shells" kids are wearing. He may even talk to YOU! Dory may visit, too. The show lasts about 10 minutes. It's totally awesome, dude!

Turtle Talk with Crush may not be offered in all of 2022.

Bruce's Sub House

Finding Nemo's Bruce the shark has a special play zone in The Seas pavilion. The Sub House has a small maze and a very large version of Bruce himself. It is so big, kids and their families can fit inside! This is a great place to take a picture, so have your camera ready. Bruce's friends Anchor and Chum are on hand for photos, too. Older kids enjoy reading all about sharks and playing games about the mighty creatures.

The Sub House may not be open in all of 2022.

HOT TIP!

Try to visit the big aquarium at 10 o'clock in the morning or at 3 in the afternoon. That's when the fish get fed. It's fun to watch! (An aquarium is a fish tank.)

JOURNEY OF WATER

Water is the star of the show at this new nature trail — just like it was in the animated film *Moana*. While guests wander pretty paths they can watch water come to life. It will leap and flow all around them!

EPCOT explorers will learn that water is on an endless journey around the world. And they will find out why the natural water cycle is so important for our planet. Journey of Water is expected to open in 2022.

THE LAND

The building called The Land looks like a big greenhouse. One of its attractions focuses on food and where it comes from. It's a boat ride called Living with the Land. The other attraction is a high-flying hang-glider ride known as Soarin' Around the World. Most kids love it. (Grown-ups do, too!)

FP+

Living with the Land

What's the most popular fruit on our planet? The banana! People eat more bananas than any other fruity snack. You will learn lots more food facts on this boat trip. The boat travels through rooms that look like a rainforest, a desert, and a prairie. Then it heads to a greenhouse area.

A recording explains all the things your boat floats past. If you are lucky, you will see some giant vegetables growing here. The greenhouse has produced some of the biggest lemons and eggplants in the world.

In all, The Land grows more than 30 tons of fruit and veggies each year. A lot of it is served to guests in EPCOT restaurants such as the Garden Grill and Coral Reef.

READER REVIEW

Living with the Land is such a cool ride. You get to learn about harvesting fruits and vegetables. It's also very cool to see how Disney is doing its part to help planet Earth.

— Kaylee (age 10), Northford, CT

HIDDEN MICKEY ALERT!

Study the paintings while you wait in line for Living with the Land. One has bubbles on it that connect to form a Mickey head.

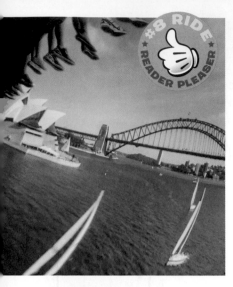

Soarin' Around the World FP+

Have you ever wondered what it's like to be a bird? To swoop and soar above the clouds? This attraction lets you do just that. In it, you will fly over natural wonders and famous sites in India, China, Australia, the U.S.A., and more.

Fasten your safety belt

Before the fun starts, you will get a seat in one of the hang gliders. Put your stuff in the basket, fasten your seat belt, sit back, and get ready.

Up, up, and away!

As your glider lifts off the ground, a movie screen lights up in front of you. On it, you'll see many different scenes. You will swoop over oceans, countrysides, and mountaintops. You'll visit sites such as the Eiffel Tower and the Great Wall of China. You may even notice different smells along the way.

Many scenes were filmed using cameras on airplanes and helicopters. Your glider moves the same way those aircraft did — so it seems as if you are really flying.

How real does it feel? Some people lift their feet because they think their toes will hit the items below! The trip takes about five minutes. If you get motion sickness or are afraid of heights, skip Soarin' Around the World.

DARK

YOU MUST BE AT LEAST
40 INCHES TALL TO RIDE
SOARIN' AROUND THE WORLD.

Awesome Planet

What is about 14 billion years old and home to nearly nine million species of living creatures? The answer is . . . Earth!

You can learn about it in a new film called *Awesome Planet*. The 10-minute movie explores the wonders of Earth and its many ecosystems. Some of the ecosystems are in trouble, but there is hope. In fact, there are many ways for us to help our planet. That's pretty awesome.

World Showcase

Anybody can be a world traveler at World Showcase. You can learn about many countries (including the U.S.A.), experience different cultures, and meet people from around the world. You can also take a trip to Arendelle — and even see Anna and Elsa.

As you visit each country, talk to the folks who work there. Some of the people in each pavilion may come from the country they represent. The pavilions were built around a lake called World Showcase Lagoon. If you make the trip all the way around the lake, you'll walk more than one mile!

Canada

If you look at a map of North America, Canada is at the top, just north of the United States. It is a beautiful country. The Canada pavilion at EPCOT is very pretty, too. There's a mountain, a stream, gardens, and a totem pole.

The highlight is a movie called *Canada Far and Wide*. The scenes completely surround you. Since you stand the whole time, it's easy to turn around and see everything. Many kids enjoy the movie but wish the theater had seats.

READER REVIEW

This pavilion shows what Canadians are proud of. I should know — I'm from Canada! I wish the film included even more, but it's a great introduction to my country.

— Shelby (age 14), Calgary, Canada

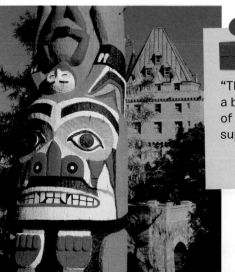

READER TIP

"There is a walking path and a big waterfall in the back of the Canada pavilion. It's super cool!"

— Judy (age 10), Greenwich, CT

HIDDEN MICKEY ALERT!

Find the totem pole in front of Canada's Northwest Mercantile. It has two Hidden Mickeys on it! HINT: They are near the top, next to the wings.

United Kingdom

From the city of London to the English countryside, this pavilion gives a varied view of the United Kingdom. Some details to look for include the smoke stains painted on the chimneys to make them appear old, and the grassy roofs that are really made of plastic broom bristles. The buildings look like those in a real British village. A rock band may play in the courtyard. And you may get a chance to meet Alice in Wonderland, Mary Poppins, and Winnie the Pooh and his pals. (They may wave from a distance.)

WHO AM I?

- My home is in Italy.
- I am a woodcarver.
- Pinocchio is my son.

Answer: Geppetto

France

The Eiffel Tower is probably the best-known landmark at the France pavilion. (The real one is in Paris, France.) The buildings look like those in a real French town. Many of the workers here come from France. They speak English with a French accent. Of course, they speak French, too! Surprise them by saying *bonjour* (pronounced: *bohn-zhoor*). It means "good day" in French.

The main attractions — besides the treats at the bakery, an ice cream shop, and a chance to see Belle — are a *Ratatouille* adventure and films called *Impressions de France* and *Beauty and the Beast Sing-Along*. The first movie takes you from one end of France to the other. It's shown on a big screen, and you get to sit down and take in the sights. The other movie lets you sing along with Belle, Lumiere, and other friends from Disney's *Beauty and the Beast*. You can read more about it below.

Beauty and the Beast Sing-Along

There are two movies in EPCOT's France pavilion. One is all about the country of France. The other tells the tale as old as time — Beauty and the Beast! This short film makes *Beauty and the Beast* fans very happy. So happy that they may feel like singing.

Spoiler alert: Le Fou played a special role in the *Beauty and the Beast* story — but it wasn't included in the movie. So viewers didn't know what a good guy he really is. This film tells you how Le Fou helped Belle and Beast become friends. Feel free to sing along with the songs in the film. If you don't know the words, don't worry — they appear on the screen.

Remy's Ratatouille Adventure

You will be shrunk to the size of a rat in EPCOT's brand-new 3-D attraction. After that, you'll scurry through Gusteau's Restaurant in a silly adventure. Expect to see characters from the movie *Ratatouille*, plus interesting sights, sounds, and smells. The ride cars twist around a bit — do not ride with a full stomach.

DARK

LOUD

Morocco

The country of Morocco is famous for works of art called mosaics (pronounced: *moe-ZAY-uks*). A mosaic is made up of many colorful tiles. That's why there is beautiful tile work on the walls of this pavilion. Moroccan artists made sure the mosaics here were done right.

The buildings are copies of monuments in Moroccan cities, including Fez and Marrakesh. There are many shops selling items you might find in Morocco. Guests can buy baskets, snacks, jewelry, fez hats, and other clothing. Princess Jasmine visits here, too.

Salam alaikum (pronounced: *sah-LAHM wah-LAY-koom*) means "hello" in Morocco. (It's in the Arabic language.)

HOT TIP!

When it is safe to perform in person, talented folks will entertain guests all over World Showcase. Will live shows happen during your visit to EPCOT? Ask a parent to check the My Disney Experience app or website to find out.

TOPIARIES

There's something odd about some of the trees and shrubs at Walt Disney World — they are shaped like Disney characters! These plants are called topiaries (pronounced: *TOE-pea-air-eez*). They are carefully grown by gardeners to create their special form. You may spot an Alice topiary by the Mad Tea Party in the Magic Kingdom, Mary Poppins at the Grand Floridian resort, and Pooh and pals in the Crystal Palace restaurant at the Magic Kingdom. In the spring, EPCOT has nearly 80 topiaries on display. How many can you find?

PHOTO BY JILL SAFRO

Japan

The giant temple out front is called a pagoda (pronounced: *puh-GO-dah*). It makes the Japanese pavilion easy to spot. It looks like a famous pagoda in the city of Nara, Japan.

Be sure to notice the evergreen trees. In Japan, they are symbols of eternal life. (Eternal means forever.) Some trees found in traditional Japanese gardens can't survive in Florida. Similar trees were used instead. They like the Florida weather!

Japanese drummers may perform outside the pagoda. The huge department store has lots of souvenirs from Japan. Would you like to say "good morning" in Japanese? Just say *ohayo gozaimasu* (pronounced: *oh-hi-yoh goh-zy-ee-mahs*).

JUST FOR KIDS!

EPCOT has something special for younger kids: Kidcot Fun Stops. There's one in each country at World Showcase — that's 11 in all! At each stop, you can collect activity cards. And you will learn how kids have fun in countries all over the world.

READER TIP

"Try to eat meals early or late in the day to avoid long lines!"

— John (age 14), Washington Township, NJ

HIDDEN MICKEY ALERT!

As you enter the lobby of The American Adventure, you will see paintings on the walls. One painting shows a wagon being pulled by oxen. There is a Hidden Mickey on the leg of one of the creatures.

The American Adventure

The United States of America is the star of this pavilion. That's why it is called The American Adventure.

The American Adventure show takes place inside a building that looks like Independence Hall (the real Independence Hall is in Philadelphia, Pennsylvania). The show celebrates the American spirit throughout the country's history.

Benjamin Franklin and Mark Twain host the show. (Ben Franklin is one of the founders of the U.S.A. And Mark Twain is one of its greatest authors.) They look so life-like, you may forget that they are mechanical. Ben Franklin even walks up a flight of stairs!

The American Adventure show honors many heroes from history: the pilgrims, Alexander Graham Bell, Jackie Robinson, Susan B. Anthony, Walt Disney, and others. It's a great way to learn about American history. It's best for older kids.

Italy

Venice is an Italian city known for waterways called canals. There are no big canals at EPCOT's Italy, but the pavilion does look a lot like the real thing. The tower is a smaller version of the Campanile, a famous building in Venice.

Take note of the gondolas (pronounced: *GAHN-doe-lahz*) tied to the dock in the lagoon. They are a type of boat used for traveling in the canals of Venice.

Say *buon giorno* (pronounced: *bwon JOR-no*). It means "good day" in Italian.

DID YOU KNOW?

The tallest building in the Italy pavilion is a bell tower. It is 83 feet tall. On top of that tower is a shiny angel statue. It is shiny because it is covered in gold leaf (gold that has been hammered into thin sheets).

INTERNATIONAL MOUSE

Mickey Mouse is famous all over the world. But not everyone knows the movie-star mouse by that name. In Italy he is called Topolino. In Greece he's known as Miky Maoye. Norwegians call him Mikke Mus. In Sweden he goes by Musse Pigg. And in China he's Mi Lao Shu. That's a lot of names for one mouse to remember!

China

Disney's version of the Temple of Heaven is at the center of this pavilion. It's a landmark in the Chinese city of Beijing. Inside, there is a Circle-Vision 360 movie called *Reflections of China*. (There are no seats in the theater.)

Before going in to the movie, look around the waiting area. It's decorated in shades of red and gold. These colors mean good luck in China.

The film takes guests on a tour of the country. It is worth seeing, but it is more popular with adults than kids. Most younger guests would rather spend their time checking out the fish in the koi pond or watching the acrobats perform in the courtyard.

The film shown in China may change in 2022. For updates, ask a parent to visit *disneyworld.com*.

One way to say "hello" in Chinese is *ni hao* (say: *nee HOW*).

READER REVIEW

I really like EPCOT's China. It has a massive gift shop, a pond with fish, and lots of food, plus a movie! I could spend a year — and a lot of money — here.

— Beckie (age 9), Gettysburg, PA

Germany

There isn't a village in Germany quite like the one at EPCOT. It's a combination of cities and small towns from all around the country. Try to stop by the pavilion on the hour so you can see the special cuckoo clock near the toy shop and hear it chime.

In German, "good day" is *guten tag* (say: *GOO-ten tahg*).

READER REVIEW

Germany is one of my favorite pavilions. I love the cuckoo clocks, teddy bears, and sausages. A great time to visit Germany is in October for Oktoberfest. There are special games, food, singing, and dancing.

— Micheline (age 9), Coral Springs, FL

HIDDEN MICKEY ALERT!

You'll find a Mickey in the grass in Germany's miniature village.

Norway

You will discover the history and culture of Norway at this pavilion. The magical kingdom of Arendelle can be discovered, too. Anna and Elsa have a summer home here!

Frozen Ever After FP+

The main building is a castle. It was based on an ancient fortress in Norway's capital city of Oslo. Inside, there is an attraction called Frozen Ever After. On this boat ride, guests travel through the beautiful (and icy) queendom of Arendelle. It includes a Summer Celebration and a visit to Elsa's Ice Palace. Expect to see friends from *Frozen* — including Anna, Elsa, Kristoff, Olaf, and Sven.

Frozen is a popular movie — and this is a very popular attraction. Get a Fastpass if you can. The ride is fun for guests of all ages. Saying "hello" is easy in Norway. It's *hallo!*

READER REVIEW

I love the movie *Frozen* and I love this ride! I like the part when you go backwards and the drop near the end. The Audio-Animatronics are very realistic.

— Lela (age 11), Hockley, TX

MEET ANNA & ELSA

What do Anna and Elsa do when they are not busy building snowmen or preparing for Coronation Day? They greet guests at the Royal Sommerhus in EPCOT's Norway pavilion! When this book was printed, the royal sisters would wave to EPCOT guests from a safe distance. Be sure to wave back. And don't forget to have your camera ready! Anna and Elsa are happy to pose in the background of your selfie.

To find this special spot, look for Norway's wooden church. The Royal Sommerhus is just to the left (on the Mexico side).

Mexico

The pyramid (say: *PEER-uh-mid*) at the Mexico pavilion is home to the Gran Fiesta Tour Starring the Three Caballeros. It is a boat trip that takes you through the country of Mexico.

The Three Caballeros are José, Panchito, and Donald (Duck, that is). They starred in a movie together way back in 1944. Now they are back together and planning to do a big show in Mexico City. But there is a problem. Donald keeps getting lost! Don't worry, there is a happy ending. This is Disney World, after all.

After the ride, you may get to meet Donald Duck. He greets guests just outside the pyramid. (Donald moves inside when the weather is rainy.) You may also catch a show by the musical group called Mariachi Cobre. The band plays songs from Latin America.

"Hello" here is *hola* (say: *OH-lah*).

HIDDEN TREASURES OF WORLD SHOWCASE

Attractions like Spaceship Earth and Test Track are easy to find. They're huge! And they are easy to spot on a park map. But EPCOT has more to offer than rides, shows, and attractions. Many World Showcase countries have rooms filled with art, historical items, and other cool treasures. Some galleries are easier to find than others. The one in Japan is in the back of the pavilion. Find it and you will see some of the country's "adorable art."

Have you ever wondered what it's like to live in the desert? Head to Morocco to find out. The American Adventure has a display of American Indian art. And in Norway, you can step inside a Stave Church to learn about Vikings. Older kids like to search for these special spots. How many can you discover?

The galleries may not be open in all of 2022.

Entertainment

EPCOT is known for its entertainment. There are usually lots of shows and special performances every day. But some shows were on pause in 2021. Will they be back for 2022? Ask a parent to check *disneyworld.com* for updates. Here is a sample of the entertainment at EPCOT.

Meet Disney Friends

EPCOT is a wonderful place to meet Disney characters. You may run into Mickey, Minnie, Pluto, Belle, Mulan, Chip, Dale, Ralph, Vanellope, Donald Duck, and more. Get a pen and your autograph book ready — or use the pages at the back of this book.

Harmonious

This is an exciting new show. It celebrates how Disney music inspires people around the world. It has fireworks, giant floats, moving fountains, lights, and lasers. The action takes place on a lake called World Showcase Lagoon. You can get a good view from anywhere around World Showcase Lagoon. The show is presented on most nights. (It might be canceled if the weather is bad.)

Serveur Amusant™

There is a wacky waiter in France. Before he takes anyone's order, he builds a giant stack of chairs. Then he climbs to the top! Okay, he isn't really a waiter. He's a talented acrobat. And he is a lot of fun to watch. Each one of his shows lasts about 20 minutes.

World Showcase Performers

There is entertainment at each pavilion in World Showcase. Highlights include acrobats in China, musicians at the Canada Mill Stage, folk singers in Mexico, a piano player in the United Kingdom, and more. There's a funny juggler in Italy. A group called The Voices of Liberty sings patriotic songs in The American Adventure pavilion. And rock concerts often take place at the America Gardens Theater near The American Adventure. Arrive early to get a seat. And feel free to clap and sing along.

Jammitors

One of the loudest and wildest shows is inside World Celebration, where musicians bang on trash cans and, sometimes, on one another. It's a blast! (The group becomes the Jammin' Chefs during EPCOT's International Food and Wine Festival — starting in summer and going through most of November.)

Where to Find Characters
at EPCOT

Disney characters love to visit EPCOT. Friends such as Mickey, Minnie, Goofy, and Pluto take turns visiting throughout the day. Wreck-It Ralph and Vanellope von Schweetz meet guests at Imagination! And Joy might show up at the new PLAY pavilion.

You may also see Disney characters such as Donald Duck, Snow White, Belle, Mulan, Jasmine, and Aurora while you wander around the **World Showcase** part of the park. Anna and Elsa are there, too.

Disney characters are always ready for a photo op. When it's safe for folks to be close to each other, Disney friends will stand near you. Until then, the characters are happy to pose in the background of your selfies. So have your camera ready and say cheese!

Details may change in 2022.

TIPS

Start your day at Test Track or Frozen Ever After, followed by Soarin' Around the World and your preferred version of Mission: SPACE. Then say hi to Nemo at The Seas with Nemo and Friends. Next, head to the Imagination pavilion.

Most of World Showcase opens at 11 A.M., but Frozen Ever After may open a bit earlier. It's in Norway.

Need a refreshing splash? Visit the Leap Frog Fountains outside the Imagination pavilion, or the squirting sidewalk near Mission: SPACE.

Go to Spaceship Earth later in the day. That is when the line for the attraction is usually the shortest.

Each World Showcase country has an activity card to share. Ask for one at the Kidcot Fun Stop. After you collect the cards, you can keep them in the Magical Memories pages of this book!

Spaceship Earth, Mission: SPACE, and Journey Into Imagination with Figment have activity zones. You can play there even if you skip the attractions. (These areas may not be open in all of 2022.)

Bring Disney pins with you so you will have something to trade with Cast Members (workers) throughout Walt Disney World. Get a parent's permission before you trade anything.

Try not to squeeze the movies at Canada, France, and China into one day. And remember — the theaters in China and Canada don't have seats.

Take time to talk to the people who work in World Showcase. Some of them come from the country of the pavilion they represent — and they have many interesting stories to tell.

At EPCOT, you can visit manatees and watch them gobble up lettuce. They eat hundreds of heads per day!

Attraction Ratings

COOL
(Check it out!)

- China (This pavilion has a movie about China.)
- Italy
- Journey Into Imagination with Figment
- United Kingdom
- Morocco
- Germany
- Japan
- Norway

VERY COOL
(Don't miss!)

- The American Adventure
- Disney and Pixar Short Film Festival
- *Awesome Planet*
- France (This pavilion has two films. One is all about France and the other is a *Beauty and the Beast* sing-along.)
- Gran Fiesta Tour (in Mexico)
- Canada (This pavilion has a movie about Canada.)
- Living with the Land

COOLEST
(See at least twice!)

- Remy's Ratatouille Adventure
- Frozen Ever After
- Soarin' Around the World
- Test Track
- Turtle Talk with Crush
- Mission: SPACE
- Spaceship Earth
- The Seas with Nemo and Friends
- Harmonious

YOUR FAVORITE EPCOT ATTRACTIONS

_____   _____

_____   _____

_____   _____

Disney's Hollywood Studios

Disney's Hollywood Studios park lets you experience imaginary worlds from movies and TV shows. There are attractions that let you ride a Slinky Dog roller coaster, sing along with Anna and Elsa, learn how to use the Force to defeat the Dark Side, see how wild stunts are performed, and a whole lot more.

The Studios park looks a little like Hollywood did back in the 1940s. Hollywood is the California city where movie-making got its big start. The Disney's Hollywood Studios park got its big start in 1989. It has shows and attractions based on *Frozen*, *Toy Story*, *Star Wars*, *The Twilight Zone*, The Muppets, and other favorites.

You will also get to see lots of characters, including Mickey, Minnie, Buzz, Woody, Olaf, Vampirina, Chewbacca, and the stars of Disney's newest films and TV shows. Be sure to have your phone or camera ready — there are plenty of surprises in store!

STAR WARS: GALAXY'S EDGE

TOY STORY LAND

N

GRAND AVE.

HOLLYWOOD BLVD.

ANIMATION COURTYARD

ECHO LAKE

SUNSET BLVD.

DISNEY'S HOLLYWOOD STUDIOS

HOLLYWOOD BOULEVARD

1. Mickey and Minnie's Runaway Railway

ECHO LAKE

2. For the First Time in Forever:
   A *Frozen* Sing-Along Celebration
3. Indiana Jones™ Epic Stunt Spectacular
4. Star Tours — The Adventures Continue
5. Mickey Shorts Theater

GRAND AVENUE

6. Muppet*Vision 3-D

STAR WARS: GALAXY'S EDGE

7. Star Wars: Rise of the Resistance
8. *Millennium Falcon*: Smugglers Run

TOY STORY LAND

9. Alien Swirling Saucers
10. Slinky Dog Dash
11. Toy Story Mania!

ANIMATION COURTYARD

12. Walt Disney Presents
13. Disney Junior Play and Dance!
14. Voyage of The Little Mermaid
15. Star Wars Launch Bay

SUNSET BOULEVARD

16. Beauty and the Beast —
    Live on Stage
17. Fantasmic!
18. The Twilight Zone™
    Tower of Terror
19. Rock 'n' Roller Coaster
20. Lightning McQueen's Racing Academy

Use this map to explore Disney's Hollywood Studios.

The Twilight Zone™ Tower of Terror

At a height of 199 feet, Tower of Terror is one of the tallest attractions at Walt Disney World. For some park guests, it is also one of the scariest.

Legend says that one Halloween night, lightning hit The Hollywood Tower Hotel. A whole section of the hotel disappeared! So did an elevator carrying five people. No one ever saw them again.

Haunted hotel

Now the hotel is haunted. If you dare to enter it, you are in for a few surprises. First, you walk through a dusty hotel lobby. Then you enter a tiny room, where Rod Serling appears on TV. (He was the host of a spooky show called *The Twilight Zone*.) Once Mr. Serling tells you the story of The Hollywood Tower Hotel, get ready — you are on your way to the Twilight Zone.

Going down!

After waiting in the boiler room, you sit down in a big elevator. The elevator takes you on a short tour of the hotel, where you see some special effects. The highlight is when the elevator cables snap. Whoosh! You plunge down eight floors!

Next, the elevator shoots up to the hotel's 13th floor. It teeters for a moment and then . . . it drops again and again at blazing speed!

WILD   SCARY   DARK

YOU MUST BE AT LEAST 40 INCHES TALL TO RIDE TOWER OF TERROR.

HOT TIP!

If you need something to hold on to while riding Tower of Terror, grab the handle next to your seat.

FP+

FP+

READER REVIEW

Three, two, one — let's rock! This is a super-fast roller coaster. It even goes upside down! Don't go on it if you are afraid of the dark or don't like going fast.

— Jayden (age 8), Orlando, FL

Rock 'n' Roller Coaster Starring Aerosmith

#3 RIDE — READER PLEASER

This ride rocks. It travels at top speed and flips you upside down! It also has a rock 'n' roll soundtrack that will have you dancing in your seat.

You're invited

Rock 'n' Roller Coaster goes really fast — it takes you from zero to 60 miles per hour in the first three seconds of the ride! You need the speed because you are on your way to an Aerosmith concert — and you are running late.

It's showtime!

The ride takes place in a stretch limousine on a roller coaster track. The limo's radio is tuned to the concert. You can hear the band warming up, but your car is not moving yet. Then, just as the concert starts, the light turns green and you're on your way. You zoom along the California highway and make it just in time for the end of the show. Hang on!

WILD SCARY DARK LOUD

YOU MUST BE AT LEAST 48 INCHES TALL TO RIDE.

Lightning McQueen's Racing Academy

Calling all *Cars* fans! What does it take to become a champion racer? Lightning McQueen wants to teach you. McQueen shares tricks of his trade with the help of a simulator and giant video screen. He is joined by pals from Radiator Springs.

After the show, guests may get to pose for a photo with Cruz Ramirez and enjoy *Cars*-themed games. Lightning McQueen's Racing Academy is in a building called Sunset Showcase. You will find it near the Rock 'n' Roller Coaster attraction.

PHOTO BY JILL SAFRO

FP+

Beauty and the Beast — Live on Stage

It's hard to keep quiet during this stage show — it makes you want to clap and sing along. The music comes straight from Disney's animated film *Beauty and the Beast*.

As the show begins, Belle is frustrated by life in her small town. She is dreaming of exciting, faraway places. Later on, she becomes a prisoner in Beast's castle. All of the castle's residents are under a magic spell. Lumiere, Cogsworth, Mrs. Potts, Chip, and the rest of the gang are there to help (and perform "Be Our Guest"). In the end, the spell is broken. Beast becomes human again.

This show may not be offered in all of 2022.

READER REVIEW

I liked the lively colors and the music in this show. I didn't like how it skipped so fast from one song to the next, because that made it more challenging to follow along, but I still got the story. It's a show the entire family can enjoy!

— Pharra (age 11), Alpharetta, GA

 DID YOU KNOW?

The first performance of Beauty and the Beast — Live on Stage took place on November 22, 1991. That was the exact same day Disney's animated version of *Beauty and the Beast* was first shown in United States movie theaters! Have you seen it?

FP+

HOT TIP!

The sidewalk by The Chinese Theater is covered with handprints and footprints. They belong to famous performers. Compare yours with those of Hollywood stars! (Wash your hands when you are done.)

WILD

HIDDEN MICKEY ALERT!

Mickey Mouse is one of the famous Hollywood stars whose footprints and handprints are on the sidewalk in front of The Chinese Theater.

Mickey and Minnie's Runaway Railway

How many cartoons have you seen in your lifetime? Hundreds? Thousands? Well, how many have you actually been IN? Probably not too many! This new attraction puts you in the middle of wild and wacky Mickey Mouse cartoons.

You're a star

At Mickey and Minnie's Runaway Railway, guests walk through a movie screen and become part of the show. Of course, you won't be alone in the crazy cartoon world — lots of Disney friends will join you on the journey.

All aboard!

The adventure begins with Mickey Mouse and Minnie Mouse preparing for a picnic. Then — TOOT! TOOT! A train chugs up and Goofy is the engineer. That's when you join the fun. Anything can happen in the cartoon world, so expect lots of surprises.

For the First Time in Forever: A Frozen Sing-Along Celebration

Have you ever heard of a song called "Let It Go"? Yes, we thought so! That is just one of the many musical numbers in the movie *Frozen*. And this is the spot to go to if you want to sing along with the characters in the film.

Singing in Arendelle

The experience happens in the Hyperion Theater. The show begins with Arendelle getting two new historians. They tell most of the *Frozen* story in a funny way. When parts of the film play on a giant screen, the audience sings along. Don't know all the words? You can read them on the big screen. Just follow the bouncing snowflake.

Anna and Elsa take the stage!

Singing with the movie is fun, but many kids think the best part is when Anna and Elsa appear live on stage. Anna shows up early, but Elsa arrives a bit later. Don't worry — it's worth the wait.

This show happens several times a day. Ask a parent to check the My Disney Experience app or website for showtimes. And get there a few minutes early. Our *Frozen* friends are quite popular.

FP+

WHO AM I?

- I love to play piano.
- I did not enjoy being Mr. Mittens.
- 22 helped save my soul.

Answer: Joe Gardner

Mickey Shorts Theater

As you probably know, Mickey Mouse likes to wear shorts. And if you're a Disney Channel fan, you know that he also stars in them. Short cartoons, that is!

There is a new Mickey cartoon playing at Disney's Hollywood Studios. It's called *Vacation Fun*. And you can have some fun watching it at the Mickey Shorts Theater — where the seats look a lot like Mickey's red shorts. The theater is next to For the First Time in Forever: A Frozen Sing-Along Celebration.

After the show, you can pose for some silly photos. The photo ops feature some popular Mickey cartoons: *Yodelburg*, *Potatoland*, *Panda-monium*, and more. Say cheese!

WONDERFUL WORLD OF ANIMATION

There is an animated adventure inside the park's Chinese Theater — Mickey and Minnie's Runaway Railway. And there's an animated adventure on the outside, too! It's called Wonderful World of Animation. It takes place on and around the theater.

The 12-minute show sends you through 90 years of Disney and Pixar animation. It is action-packed! The fun begins with a little guy you know well — the one and only Mickey Mouse! All your favorites are included, from *Aladdin* to *Zootopia*. You may have to see it twice to catch it all.

To get a good view, stand in front of the theater. Don't stand right next to a speaker — this show can be loud! And remember: "It all started with a mouse."

Wonderful World of Animation was on pause in 2021. Will it be presented during your visit in 2022? Ask a parent to visit *disneyworld.com* to find out.

Disney Junior Play and Dance!

Are you a Disney Junior fan? If so, head straight to this attraction. Friends from Disney Junior programs will dance and sing with you in a stage show. Expect to find favorite characters from shows like *Vampirina*, *The Lion Guard*, and *Doc McStuffins*. Mickey Mouse is there, too!

Have a seat on the floor

As you enter the theater, you may notice something strange — there are no seats. But don't worry. The carpet is comfy, so sit down and make yourself at home. (There are a few benches in the back of the theater. Grown-ups like to sit on them.)

A big hit with little guests

Big kids may get a kick out of Disney Junior Play and Dance, but young kids seem to have the most fun here. If you have little brothers or sisters, take them to this show.

Mickey and Minnie Starring in Red Carpet Dreams

It's no secret that Mickey Mouse and Minnie Mouse are big Hollywood stars. And they have invited you to meet them backstage at Disney's Hollywood Studios — at a special building on Commissary Lane. Inside, Minnie looks like she is ready for a fancy party or awards show. Mickey is decked out in his magical outfit from *Fantasia*. (In that film, he plays the Sorcerer's Apprentice.)

Both mice are happy to see their fans and pose for photos — because that's what friendly movie stars do. Say hi to Mickey and Minnie for us!

This area may not be offered in all of 2022. Will it be open when you visit the park? Ask a parent to check *disneyworld.com* to find out.

READER REVIEW

If you're a Little Mermaid fan, this attraction is a must! The only bad part? The seats are low. Try not to sit behind people who are very tall.

— Jessica (age 12), Williamsville, NY

LOUD   SCARY   DARK

Voyage of The Little Mermaid

You don't have to be a fish to have fun underwater — and this show proves it. In it, you go below the ocean's surface with Ariel and her friends from *The Little Mermaid*. They sing and act out the story on a stage. Ariel and Eric star along with puppets, including Flounder, Sebastian, and other sea creatures.

Under the sea

There are some special effects that draw you into the show. A screen of water makes it seem like the theater really is under the sea. Lasers flash, lightning strikes, and mist sprays the audience. Scenes from the movie are shown on a big screen behind the stage.

A winning combination

The mix of people, puppets, and special effects makes for a nice show. To get the best view of all the action, try sitting toward the back of the theater. From there, the puppets look like they are really swimming.

This show may not be offered in all of 2022.

FP+

PHOTO BY JILL SAFRO

Walt Disney Presents

You probably know a lot about Mickey Mouse — he has a pup named Pluto, he loves red shorts, and Minnie Mouse is his favorite gal. But how much do you know about the man who gave Mickey to the world? You can learn a lot about Walt Disney at this attraction. He is the man who created Mickey Mouse and The Walt Disney Company.

Take your time

Some of Walt's real belongings are on display here. Look for special items such as Disney family photos, Walt's desk, and the Academy Award he won for *Snow White and the Seven Dwarfs*. Spend time exploring the exhibits before you see the film about Walt.

Fun fact

Did you know that Mickey Mouse wasn't Walt's first famous cartoon character? A rabbit named Oswald was. (That's him below — with his friend Ortensia). Walt's plans for Oswald didn't quite work out. Luckily, he did not give up, or he never would have created Mickey! To learn more about Walt Disney, turn to page 8.

READER REVIEW

Walt Disney Presents is a wonderful exhibit. It really helps you get to know Walt Disney and the magic that he brought to the world.

— Jennifer (age 12), Salina, KS

PHOTO BY JILL SAFRO

READER REVIEW

I love rides and I love arcades—so the combination of the two in Toy Story Mania makes this one of my favorite attractions. I recommend it for older kids and adults.

— Miriam (age 9), Monsey, NY

HOT TIP!

Toy Story Mania usually has a long line. If Fastpass is offered during your trip, use it. Or get there as the park opens in the morning.

Toy Story Mania!

If you think Buzz Lightyear's Space Ranger Spin is a blast, you will love Toy Story Mania! It's like jumping into a life-size video game. It also makes you feel like you're the size of a toy as you travel through colorful rooms and stop in front of screens filled with targets.

This high-tech ride has a twist: All guests wear 3-D glasses. That makes all of the special effects really pop. As you rack up points and trigger surprises, you'll be cheered on by Woody, Buzz, Jessie, Rex, Hamm, and lots of other Toy Story friends.

Toy Story Mania is good for gamers of all ages and skill levels. So if you are a beginner, you'll get better each time you play. In fact, we are pretty sure you will be giving pointers to your parents.

Slinky Dog Dash

If you've seen the movie *Toy Story*, you know that Andy is a very creative kid. But did you know he could build a roller coaster? Yep, Andy used his trusty roller coaster kit to build Slinky Dog Dash — a super fun attraction in the park's Toy Story Land.

Andy's creation lets guests ride in a car that looks exactly like Slinky Dog. The cars dash along a brightly colored track that twists around Andy's backyard. This adventure is much tamer than Rock 'n' Roller Coaster, but it's still a ride on the wild side. Guests of all ages enjoy it.

PHOTO BY JILL SAFRO

#15 RIDE — READER PLEASER

FP+

WILD

SCARY

YOU MUST BE AT LEAST 38 INCHES TALL TO RIDE SLINKY DOG DASH.

READER REVIEW

SLINKY DOG DASH IS THE BEST! I love the drops and the thrills. It's definitely wild. It isn't scary, though. Older kids and younger kids will enjoy this ride.

— Evelyn (age 9), Leesburg, VA

FP+

PHOTO BY JILL SAFRO

Alien Swirling Saucers

Andy won a space-toy playset at the Pizza Planet Arcade — and he wants to share it with you. Just climb inside a rocket-shaped toy and get ready to swirl. The rocket will be pulled by a flying saucer and an alien from *Toy Story*. Don't worry — the Little Green Men are great pilots. (And the rockets do not leave the ground.) While you spin around the galaxy, you will be treated to peppy music and lighting effects.

LOUD

YOU MUST BE AT LEAST 32 INCHES TALL TO RIDE ALIEN SWIRLING SAUCERS.

LOUD

HOT TIP!

The Indiana Jones Epic Stunt Spectacular is a noisy show. If explosions and other loud noises hurt your ears, sit in the back of the theater. It's not as loud there.

READER TIP

"Outside of Indiana Jones, there is a sign that says: DO NOT PULL THE ROPE. Ignore the sign and pull that rope! You'll be glad you did."

— Cameron (age 10), Naples, FL

Indiana Jones Epic Stunt Spectacular

Fire, explosions, daring escapes, and other special effects are the stars of this attraction. Stunt people act out scenes from the movie *Raiders of the Lost Ark* and show how special effects are done. The audience watches from a large theater, and grown-ups are picked to perform with the pros.

Fun for everyone

All the surprises keep everyone on the edge of their seats. One of the best parts of the show is the re-creation of a scene in the movie where a giant boulder rolls down and seems to crush Indiana Jones. Even though you know it's a stunt, it seems quite real.

Don't try this at home

Expert stunt people act out the scenes and explain how each of the stunts was done. They make it look very easy, but it is not. Don't try this at home!

This show may not be offered in all of 2022.

FP+

PHOTO BY JILL SAFRO

FP+

Muppet*Vision 3-D

Don't miss this attraction — it is one of the park's funniest. It begins with a wacky pre-show starring Fozzie Bear, Gonzo, Scooter, and Sam Eagle. Then you go into a theater that looks just like the one from Jim Henson's *The Muppet Show*. Here, you will see 3-D movie effects mixed with some other tricks.

Amazing effects

Some of the effects are so good that it's hard to tell what's part of the movie and what's real. During Miss Piggy's big song, bubbles look like they are inches away from you. Don't be surprised if they really are!

Look around the theater

Look all around you while you watch the show. Some of the best action happens off the screen. Be sure to look for the Swedish Chef. He is cooking up a crazy plan in the back of the theater.

DID YOU KNOW?

3-D glasses make a different picture for each of your eyes. Your brain combines those pictures and presto: 3-D! It's everyday magic. Your eyes and brain team up to make 3-D images all day. And each eye never sees the exact same thing. Test it: Point at something. Look with one eye, then the other. What happens?

Star Tours — The Adventures Continue

If you've ever been to Star Tours before, you should come back soon — it's a little different almost every time. The journey through the galaxy makes guests feel like they are part of a Star Wars movie. Before the trip, put on the special glasses — this adventure is in 3-D. Keep your eye out for Princess Leia, Darth Vader, Yoda, Finn, and BB-8.

It feels real

The ride takes place on a flight simulator — the same type used to train astronauts and pilots. Together, the simulator and movie make it feel like you are really zooming through space.

Hang on tight

The Star Tours adventure has sharp turns and lots of bumpy thrills. Do not eat anything just before you enter the attraction.

WILD   DARK   LOUD

YOU MUST BE AT LEAST 40 INCHES TALL TO RIDE STAR TOURS.

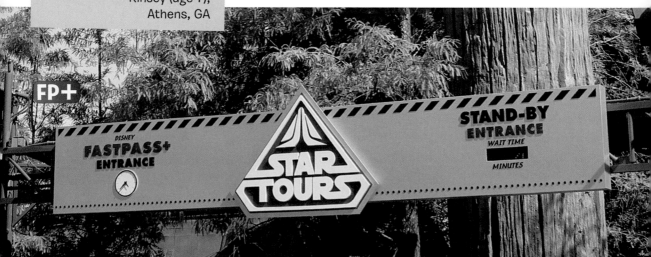

PLAY DISNEY PARKS APP

Play Disney Parks is a free mobile app that can add extra fun to your Disney trip. It has games to play while waiting in lines for shows and attractions. It tests your Disney smarts with trivia questions. And it has games that let you interact with some theme park attractions. You can play with friends and family — but be sure to ask a parent for permission to download the app.

The app offers adventures for all Disney World theme parks. One of the best spots to use it is in Star Wars: Galaxy's Edge. It can translate words written in Aurebesh— the language of the planet Batuu. You'll also be able to find hidden items in the land and hack into droids!

Always ask a parent before you use the Play Disney Parks app. And make sure you have a extra battery pack.

Jedi Training: Trials of the Temple

Calling all Padawans — you can become a Junior Jedi and defend the galaxy at Jedi Training: Trials of the Temple. It's open to kids between the ages of 4 and 12. All trainees wear brown Jedi robes and recite the Jedi Oath. They also learn how to use the Force and a lightsaber. A Jedi Master shares tricks and teaches Junior Jedi Knights how to defend against the Dark Side.

If you just want to watch the lesson, head to the stage a few minutes before showtime. If you want to be in the show, sign up at the Indiana Jones Adventure Outpost. (It is between the Indiana Jones Epic Stunt Spectacular and the 50's Prime Time Cafe.) Guests should arrive early in the day to reserve a spot in Jedi Training: Trials of the Temple. (Even if you are not in the show, it is still fun to watch.) May the Force be with you!

Afterward, robes and lightsabers are returned to the Jedi Master. Each show is about 20 minutes long.

This show may not be offered in all of 2022.

HOT TIP!

Jedi Training: Trials of the Temple takes place on a stage near an attraction called Star Tours — The Adventures Continue. The stage is outdoors, so the show may be canceled if the weather is bad.

Star Wars Launch Bay

The Launch Bay is a walk-through attraction that celebrates the stories and characters of the Star Wars universe. At the entrance, guests may head to the Launch Bay Theater. There guests view a film about Star Wars movies. It's a look at old favorites and a peek into the future.

Look at that lightsaber

Parts of the Launch Bay are like a museum filled with props, costumes, and other Star Wars items. Guests enjoy a close-up look at Stormtrooper helmets, lightsabers, and more. There's a spider bike from *Return of the Jedi* and a copy of Rey's speeder from *The Force Awakens.*

Meet Chewie

Launch Bay also has a space to meet characters from Star Wars movies. Would you like to see Chewbacca, BB-8, or Darth Vader? Here's your chance! (Characters may take turns throughout the day.)

The Launch Bay may not be open in all of 2022.

PHOTO BY JILL SAFRO

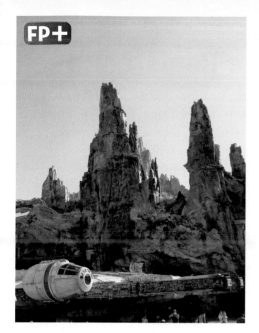

FP+

Millennium Falcon: Smugglers Run

Would you like to fly on the fastest ship in the galaxy? This exciting attraction lets you do just that. In it, you'll work with a team to complete a mission. You may get to be the pilot, fire blasters, or prepare the ship for hyperspace.

Hondo is the boss

Hondo Ohnaka is the space pirate we first met in *Star Wars: The Clone Wars*. Now he runs smuggling missions on the planet Batuu. And he wants you to work for him!

Do your job

The action takes place on the *Millennium Falcon*. It's a spaceship with room for six crew members. And each one has a job to do. If you do your job well, you will score points. If you bang up the ship, you will lose points — and land on Hondo's naughty list. You don't want that. Good luck!

HOT TIP!

Two pilots sit in the front row of the *Millennium Falcon*. The pilot on the left moves it from side to side. The pilot on the right moves the ship up and down — and sends the ship speeding into hyperspace!

SCARY

WILD

DARK

LOUD

YOU MUST BE AT LEAST 38 INCHES TALL TO RIDE SMUGGLERS RUN.

WHO AM I?

- There is a number in my name.
- I am a droid.
- That's me on page 96!

Answer: BB-8

Star Wars: Rise of the Resistance

What happens when Star Wars bad guys and good guys end up on the same planet? Well, when that planet is Batuu, a battle breaks out. The First Order and the Resistance are here — and they do NOT get along. When they begin an epic battle, guests like you will be in the middle of the action.

A wild ride

Rise of the Resistance includes fast movement, quick stops, and sharp turns. Don't ride on a full stomach!

May the Force be with you

Will you be captured by the evil First Order? Don't worry. The Force is strong in this park. If you change your mind at the last minute, ask a Cast Member to point you to an exit.

SCARY   WILD   DARK

LOUD

YOU MUST BE AT LEAST 40 INCHES TALL TO RIDE STAR WARS: RISE OF THE RESISTANCE.

WELCOME TO THE PLANET BATUU

There is a world within Walt Disney World — and it is inside Disney's Hollywood Studios. When guests visit Star Wars: Galaxy's Edge, they go to a planet called Batuu (say: *Bah-TOO*).

Batuu is very different from Earth. Many years ago, it was a busy place for traders and explorers. But those days are long gone. Now it is visited by a lot of folks on the wrong side of the law. Space pirates, smugglers, and other criminals love it here. So do people trying to avoid the evil First Order. Are you one of them?

Guests who travel here visit a place called Black Spire Outpost. It has shops, snack spots, and two attractions — Star Wars: Rise of the Resistance and *Millennium Falcon*: Smugglers Run. You may even spot some of your favorite characters (good and bad) from the Star Wars universe.

By the way, nobody says hello on Batuu. They say "bright suns!"

Entertainment

Lights! Camera! Action! There is a lot of entertainment at Disney's Hollywood Studios. Most of it has a TV or movie theme. A few of the best shows are described below. (Some shows may not happen in 2022.)

DARK SCARY LOUD

Fantasmic!

What does Mickey Mouse dream about? You can find out at Fantasmic! It's a nighttime show that combines water, lights, Disney characters, movies, music, and a little magic.

Mickey's dreams are fun to watch — but some are a little scary. (Disney villains turn his dreams into nightmares.) In the end, good wins over evil, and Mickey's dreams are happy once more.

Fantasmic is shown in a theater beside a lake. It's very popular, so be sure to line up at least an hour before showtime. And, if it isn't summer, take a jacket or a sweater — it can get chilly. If you sit near the front, you might get a little bit wet. The lake gets lit on fire, too. (It's a cool effect, but it may scare small kids.) On what nights is Fantasmic performed? Ask a parent to visit *disneyworld.com* to find out.

Citizens of Hollywood

If you take a walk on Hollywood or Sunset boulevard, you might run into performers called Citizens of Hollywood. They play the parts of movie stars, police, cab drivers, reporters, and other funny characters from the 1930s and 1940s. They love to talk to theme park guests, so don't be shy. You'll feel like you are a part of the show.

Star Wars:
A Galactic Spectacular

The park ends some nights with Star Wars–themed fireworks. The show has bursts of color, lively music, and special effects. The spectacular is presented during busy times of year. It may not be offered during your visit. Ask a parent to check *disneyworld.com* for updates.

Where to Find Characters
at Disney's Hollywood Studios

There are plenty of places to see Disney and Pixar characters at Disney's Hollywood Studios. Mickey and Minnie greet folks in different rooms at a place called **Mickey and Minnie Starring in Red Carpet Dreams**. You will find everyone's favorite snowman, Olaf, in the **Celebrity Spotlight** building. (These spots may not be open in all of 2022.)

Pluto and Disney Junior characters such as Vampirina, Fancy Nancy, and Doc McStuffins appear in **Animation Courtyard**. Friends and foes from Star Wars visit **Star Wars Launch Bay** and the park's newest land, **Star Wars: Galaxy's Edge**. (Watch out for Stormtroopers!)

Jessie, Woody, and Buzz Lightyear greet park guests in **Toy Story Land**. The Green Army soldiers perform in Toy Story Land. The green soldiers may play games, too!

Disney characters love a good photo op. When it's safe for folks to be close, Disney friends will stand near you. Until then, characters are happy to pose in the background of selfies. So have your camera ready and say cheese!

Details may change in 2022.

TIPS

Arrive at Disney's Hollywood Studios before the opening time. The gates often open a few minutes ahead of the scheduled time.

Some shows may not open until late morning. Check a Tip Board or the My Disney Experience app for show times.

Do you like to search for Hidden Mickeys? Go to the Mickey and Minnie's Runaway Railway attraction. It has dozens of Hidden Mickeys to discover!

Some folks think the number 13 is scary. But if the wait time at Tower of Terror is 13 minutes, there is probably a shorter wait — and that's not scary at all!

There are "chicken exits" at both Tower of Terror and Rock 'n' Roller Coaster, just in case you change your mind at the last minute.

The front rows at Fantasmic get a little wet. The best seats are in the back at either end of the theater.

The attractions in Toy Story Land and Star Wars: Galaxy's Edge are popular. Ask a parent to reserve Fastpass+ assignments if they are available.

Don't eat just before riding Rock 'n' Roller Coaster, Slinky Dog Dash, *Millennium Falcon*: Smugglers Run, Star Wars: Rise of the Resistance, Alien Swirling Saucers, Tower of Terror, or Star Tours.

Attraction Ratings

COOL
(Check it out!)

- Celebrity Spotlight (meet Olaf)

- Disney Junior Play and Dance!

- Lightning McQueen's Racing Academy

- Mickey & Minnie Starring in Red Carpet Dreams

- Walt Disney Presents

- Jedi Training: Trials of the Temple

- Star Wars Launch Bay

- Voyage of The Little Mermaid

VERY COOL
(Don't miss!)

- Alien Swirling Saucers

- Beauty and the Beast — Live on Stage

- Fantasmic!

- For the First Time in Forever: A Frozen Sing-Along Celebration

- Mickey Shorts Theater

- Star Wars: A Galactic Spectacular (fireworks)

- Indiana Jones Epic Stunt Spectacular

- Muppet*Vision 3-D

COOLEST
(See at least twice!)

- Mickey and Minnie's Runaway Railway

- Toy Story Mania!

- Slinky Dog Dash

- The Twilight Zone Tower of Terror

- *Millennium Falcon*: Smugglers Run

- Rock 'n' Roller Coaster Starring Aerosmith

- Star Wars: Rise of the Resistance

- Star Tours — The Adventures Continue

YOUR FAVORITE HOLLYWOOD STUDIOS ATTRACTIONS

_____ _____

_____ _____

_____ _____

Disney's Animal Kingdom

Disney's Animal Kingdom celebrates animals of every kind, from lions, tigers, and zebras to giant turtles whose ancestors lived during the time of the dinosaurs. And they're all real! You may get closer to them than you've ever been before. There are dinosaurs, too. The dinos aren't real, but they sure seem to be.

Animal Kingdom is a theme park with many shows and attractions. Just as in the Magic Kingdom, there are different "lands" to visit in Disney's Animal Kingdom. The park's major lands are called Discovery Island, Asia, Africa, DinoLand U.S.A., and Pandora — The World of Avatar.

All guests enter the park through The Oasis. It's like a jungle. It has lots of plants and a few wild animals. Take some time to look around. Then cross a bridge to Discovery Island, admire the giant Tree of Life, and decide which land to explore first.

Some of the park's shows and attractions were on pause in 2021. Many will return in 2022. What will be open during your visit? Ask a parent to check *disneyworld.com* to find out!

DISNEY'S ANIMAL KINGDOM

N

4

2

3

1

AFRICA

5

9

10

11

ASIA

12

7

6

8

DISCOVERY ISLAND

14

15

THE OASIS

DINOLAND U.S.A.

16

17

PANDORA—
THE WORLD OF AVATAR

18

13

ENTRANCE PLAZA

AFRICA
1. Kilimanjaro Safaris
2. Gorilla Falls
   Exploration Trail
3. Wildlife Express Train to
   Rafiki's Planet Watch
4. Rafiki's Planet Watch
5. Festival of the Lion King

DISCOVERY ISLAND
6. The Tree of Life
7. Discovery Island Trails
8. It's Tough to Be a Bug!

ASIA
9. UP! A Great Bird Adventure
10. Maharajah Jungle Trek
11. Kali River Rapids
12. Expedition Everest

DINOLAND U.S.A.
13. Dinosaur
14. The Boneyard playground
15. Finding Nemo — The Musical
16. Chester & Hester's Dino-Rama!

PANDORA—THE WORLD OF AVATAR
17. Avatar Flight of Passage
18. Na'vi River Journey

What's the best way to see Animal Kingdom? Use this map to help you decide.

Discovery Island

Discovery Island is the gateway to all the other lands in the park. The Tree of Life stands near the center of Discovery Island. If you wander near its roots, you will see different kinds of creatures.

The Tree of Life

This human-made tree is 145 feet tall. From far away it looks like any other tree. But when you get up close, you will see that this is not an ordinary tree. It's covered with animals!

Artists have carved 325 animal images into its trunk. In fact, it's called The Tree of Life because it's covered with so many different kinds of animal life. The lion is easy to see. Other animals, such as the ant and dolphin, are a lot harder to spot. How many can you find? Some kids like to use binoculars to peek at the animals. There is another good way to get a close-up view of the Tree of Life. Just take a short walk along the Discovery Island Trail. It leads to the tree's giant trunk.

READER REVIEW

Once inside Animal Kingdom, you can't miss The Tree of Life. Trying to spot all the animals on the tree is nearly impossible! A great place to search for animals is while in line for It's Tough to Be a Bug!

— John (age 14), Washington Township, NJ

PHOTO BY MIKE CARROLL

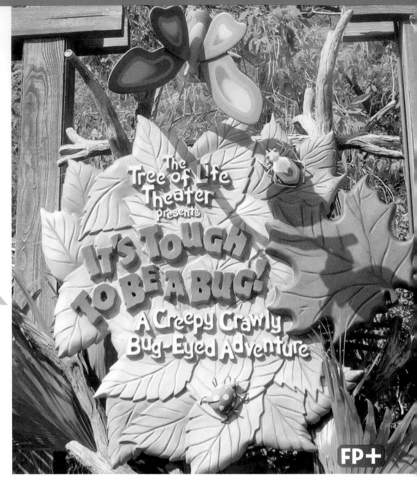

FP+

PHOTO BY JILL SAFRO

READER REVIEW

I am not a big fan of insects, so I found this show very suspenseful. You never know where the bugs are going to pop up next! The effects are great, right down to the Audio-Animatronics Flik and Hopper.

— Benjamin (age 11), East Providence, RI

HOT TIP!

If you hate creepy crawlers, avoid It's Tough to Be a Bug!

READER TIP

"At It's Tough to Be a Bug, be sure to sit back straight in your chair so you don't miss a thing."

— Chelsea (age 12), Howell, NJ

LOUD   SCARY   DARK

It's Tough to Be a Bug!

The Tree of Life has a hollow trunk. It's cool and roomy inside. That makes it a great place to watch a 3-D movie called It's Tough to Be a Bug! It's hosted by Flik, the star of A Bug's Life. Most of these bugs are friendly and funny. But when the evil Hopper makes an appearance, the show gets a little bit scary.

This movie is about the tiny creatures that outnumber all others on our planet — bugs. In it, animated insects use music and special effects to show how hard their lives are. They also try to show humans just how important bugs really are. This show is much too scary for some kids.

DinoLand U.S.A.

The entrance to this land is marked by a bridge and a dinosaur skeleton. Inside, you may discover life-like dinosaurs and animals that have existed since prehistoric times. The main attraction is called Dinosaur, but there are lots of other things to see and do. For a hand-clapping good time, catch Finding Nemo — The Musical. In DinoLand you can also dig for bones in a playground, learn about real dinosaurs, or spin on a friendly dino ride.

PHOTO BY JILL SAFRO

Chester and Hester's Dino-Rama!

Dino-Rama is an area in DinoLand U.S.A. It looks like a dinosaur-themed fair, complete with carnival games and one ride. (It costs money to play the games, but you can enjoy the attraction as much as you want without paying an extra penny.)

HIDDEN MICKEY ALERT!

First, find the old gas pump in Chester and Hester's Dino-Rama. Then look at the ground near the pump. You just may spot a Hidden Mickey in the cracks!

TriceraTop Spin

The dinos that soar on this ride look like they're part of a wind-up toy. Just like at Dumbo the Flying Elephant and the Magic Carpets of Aladdin, riders here can control how high or low they go. Younger kids love this attraction.

READER REVIEW

No more Dinosaur for me! You heard me right — even at my age (10), this ride is too dark, wild, loud, and bumpy. If you like rides like that, you may like Dinosaur. But it is too stressful for me.

— Maria (age 10),
Katy, TX

READER TIP

"Dinosaur is very loud and dark, and it really jerks and pulls you around. Some young kids won't like it at all!"

— Julia (age 11),
Prairieville, LA

DID YOU KNOW?

The residents of Animal Kingdom and Disney's Animal Kingdom Lodge are very hungry critters. Together, they gobble up about 10,000 pounds of food each day! The meals come from a special group of experts called the Animal Nutrition Team.

Dinosaur

This thrilling and scary ride takes guests back to the last few minutes of the Earth's Cretaceous Period. (That is when the dinosaurs died out.)

Save the dinosaur

The mission on Dinosaur is to save the last iguanodon. You have to brave a meteor shower and one of the largest Audio-Animatronics creatures Disney has ever made. It is a dinosaur called a carnotaurus, and it may be the scariest thing you've ever seen. This monster has the face of a toad, horns like a bull, and squirrel-like arms. It looks like it's alive. The nostrils even move as it breathes. And, boy, can it run. The carnotaurus runs for about 30 feet. Be careful. The creature is not just after the iguanodon — it wants to eat you, too!

An exciting (and scary) ride

Most kids agree that this is a very exciting ride, but one that might not be for everyone. Kids who don't enjoy scary rides can find some tamer dinos on TriceraTop Spin. But for kids who like to be scared, Dinosaur is a must.

LOUD

SCARY

DARK

WILD

YOU MUST BE AT LEAST 40 INCHES TALL TO RIDE DINOSAUR.

#20 RIDE
READER PLEASER

FP+

Finding Nemo — The Musical

Uh-oh. Nemo has wandered off again. Will he ever learn? We hope not, since this show tells his story in a whole new way — with music. There are lots of peppy tunes to sing along with during the performance. High-flying acrobats, colorful puppets, and talented dancers round out the show.

The action takes place in DinoLand's Theater in the Wild. The show happens inside a building, but it seems like it's under water. You won't get wet, though, since it's all done with special effects.

The 40-minute show is presented several times a day. It is popular — try to arrive early. The theater is air-conditioned, so you can cool off while Nemo and his friends entertain. The show is a bit long for young kids. It may not be offered in 2022.

FP+

HOT TIP!

Finding Nemo — The Musical is a popular show. Plan to arrive about 30 minutes early to get a good seat.

READER REVIEW

I don't love stage shows that much — but the giant fish are pretty neat! Overall, I think Finding Nemo — The Musical is best for Nemo fans.

— Riley (age 12), Dayton, OH

WILDERNESS EXPLORERS

In the movie UP, Russell is a dedicated Wilderness Explorer. He wants to earn as many merit badges as he can. Now you can become a Wilderness Explorer, too. Start by heading to Wilderness Explorer Headquarters at the Oasis bridge. After you take the official pledge, you will get a book that describes different challenges. Complete a challenge to earn a sticker badge! There are about 30 different badges in all. There is no extra charge to become an Animal Kingdom Wilderness Explorer, and the stickers are free. It's fun for the whole family.

The Boneyard

Are you ready to jump into the biggest sandbox you've ever seen? It's here, and it's filled with bones! You can uncover the bones of a mammoth and find clues about how the animal died.

There are also dinosaur footprints that roar when you jump in them and a big xylophone that looks like dinosaur bones. There's a rope maze for climbing and slides to slip down, too. Be sure to check out the Olden-Gate Bridge. It looks like a dinosaur skeleton.

The Boneyard may be closed for parts of 2022.

READER REVIEW

My brother is 5 years old and he had a better time at The Boneyard than I did. There's lots to do, but I couldn't wait to ride Dinosaur!

— Olivia (age 9), Watertown, WI

HOT TIP!

The xylophone is next to the trunk in The Boneyard playground. Press the bones to make a sound.

WHO AM I?

- My hair is long and silky.
- I have a hook.
- I like Hei Hei — in my belly!

Answer: Maui

Africa

Before creating this land, Disney Imagineers spent months in Africa. They learned all about its plants and animals. When they came home, they created an African forest and a grassland in Florida. And they filled it with hundreds of the same animals they had seen in Africa. Most of the animals in Animal Kingdom came from special parks and zoos around the world. You can see many animals on a safari ride and learn all about them at Rafiki's Planet Watch.

#19 RIDE
READER PLEASER

FP+

PHOTO BY JILL SAFRO

Kilimanjaro Safaris

In this wild adventure, you ride in a vehicle that is wide open. There's almost nothing between you and the animals. You may see hippos, lions, giraffes, rhinos, elephants, and more. Some animals may even come up close. But don't worry — dangerous animals can't get near you. It is perfectly safe. You can go on a safari during the day and at night. The animals are always there.

This attraction got a new addition a few years back — zebras! Keep your eyes peeled for these beautiful creatures. And have your camera ready at all times. You can take a lot of interesting photos in these parts.

READER REVIEW

Kilimanjaro Safaris lets you see animals that you never thought you would see in person. I saw lions, rhinos, crocodiles, and much more! I like this ride because I want to become a scientist.

— Samuel (age 8), North Chili, NY

Gorilla Falls Exploration Trail

After you take a ride on Kilimanjaro Safaris, go for a walk in the Pangani Forest. This nature trail has a lot to discover. You may come across a grazing zebra or spot some hippos in a watering hole. And you are sure to see hundreds of fish and birds in the aviary. (Say: *AY-vee-air-ee.*)

No binoculars necessary

Pick up a bird guide (in the aviary) and see how many different birds you can spot. Afterward, make a stop at the meerkat exhibit. Some people call it the "Timon exhibit" because he's a meerkat. (There are no Pumbaas here. Meerkats and warthogs don't get along well in real life.)

Snoop on the troop

At the end of the trail, you may see a troop of gorillas. They are usually hiding out or playing on the hills.

It takes about 25 minutes to see everything on this trail.

READER REVIEW

I love to see all the animals on this trail after we ride the safari. I even got to see a baby gorilla.

There are lots of paths to follow — stay close to your adult. This is fun for everyone.

— Zoe (age 7), Birmingham, AL

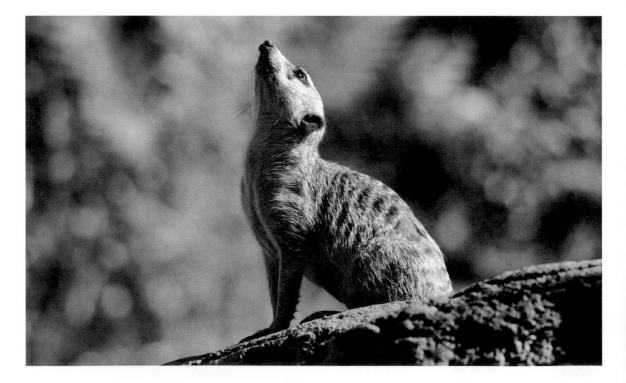

Rafiki's Planet Watch

A train called the Wildlife Express is the only way to get to Rafiki's Planet Watch. (Hop aboard in Africa.) During the 7-minute ride, you get a peek at the buildings where animals from the safari ride are cared for.

Conservation Station

After a brief train trip, guests walk on a nature trail to reach Conservation Station. Inside, you can watch as veterinarians treat animal patients. You can spy on snakes and tarantulas in the Reptile Room. (Don't worry, the creepy critters are all behind glass!) You can get a nice view of experts preparing meals for hungry critters, and much more.

Lend a helping hand

Rafiki's Planet Watch teaches you all about animals — and what people can do to help them. There are even ways to find out about conservation projects near your home.

Guests can visit with goats and sheep in an area called Affection Section. It is okay to pet them, but feeding is not allowed. Wash your hands after your visit.

HOT TIP!

Rafiki's Planet Watch closes before the rest of the park. Ask a Cast Member or check the My Disney Experience app for the closing time — and plan to spend at least an hour there.

THE ANIMATION EXPERIENCE

Do you enjoy Disney's animated films? Have you ever wondered how they are made? Now is your chance to find out. Head to Conservation Station for the Animation Experience. It's a class taught by a real Disney animator. In it, you will see how Disney artists study real animals to create characters. And you'll learn how to draw your own version of a popular Disney character.

This class may not be offered in all of 2022.

DID YOU KNOW?

Disney's Animal Kingdom is home to more than 2,000 live creatures and about 300 animal species. Quite a few plants live there, too. In fact, the park has more than four million trees, shrubs, flowers, and other plants!

Festival of the Lion King

This is one spectacular musical show. Even if you have the movie memorized, you are in for a few surprises. Many characters from the film are here, but they look a bit different. Most of them are played by humans dressed in colorful costumes.

An action-packed performance

The theater has big stages that look like parade floats. (That's because they were once in a parade at Disneyland.) On one, Simba sits atop Pride Rock. Pumbaa sits on another. Gymnasts dressed like monkeys jump and do tricks.

The mighty jungle

After singers and dancers perform songs from *The Lion King*, it is time for the big finish. Stilt walkers, acrobats, and dancers join Timon for the song "The Lion Sleeps Tonight." Even the audience gets in on the act, so get ready to clap and sing!

Parts of this show may be different in 2022.

LOUD

WHO AM I?

- I'm blue.
- Nemo is my pal.
- I speak whale!

Answer: Dory

Asia

Asia is the largest continent on Earth. It's almost twice as big as North America! The land called Asia in Animal Kingdom is a lot smaller than the real thing, but it gives you an idea of what the Asian continent is like. It has jungles and rainforests and amazing animals. It's also home to a raging river. You can whirl down the river on a raft ride called Kali River Rapids. For one of the most exciting experiences of all, ride Expedition Everest. And check out an awesome bird show. It's a real hoot!

Maharajah Jungle Trek

Put on your walking shoes and keep your eyes open. This trail is the place to spot scaly critters called Komodo dragons, plus deer, giant fruit bats (they eat melon), and tigers. You'll also see colorful birds along the way and tons of plants and trees. Check the map at the trail's entrance to know what to look for.

You see the bats about halfway through your walk. Their wings are enormous! In some places, there is no glass between you and the bats. Don't worry — they're not interested in humans. Still, it might be creepy to stand so close to them. If the bats make you uncomfortable, there's a window outside the building that lets you watch them from a distance.

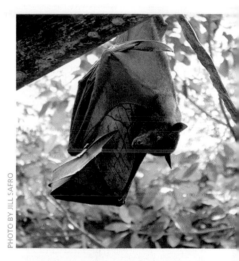

PHOTO BY JILL SAFRO

HIDDEN MICKEY ALERT!

When you visit the Maharajah Jungle Trek, look for wall art near the tigers. You'll find Hidden Mickeys on it!

READER REVIEW

Expedition Everest is awesome! It has enough thrill to last you a week. I love how it tells a story. Even while waiting in line, it keeps you on your toes! This ride is better for older kids. Little kids might find it scary.

— Mary (age 11), Bexley, OH

READER TIP

"Remember to bring a water bottle with you to Animal Kingdom on hot days."

— Meg (age 12), Vero Beach, FL

Expedition Everest

Mount Everest is the tallest mountain in the world. Can you guess the name of the tallest mountain in Walt Disney World? If you said Expedition Everest, you are right! Of course, it is much more than a mountain. It's a thrilling train ride through forests and waterfalls and over snow-capped mountain peaks. This ride is a lot rougher than Big Thunder Mountain Railroad. Here, you not only travel forward and backward through caverns and canyons, you also pass an angry yeti (that's an abominable snowman). His job is to protect the mountain from you!

This attraction is not for everyone. If you love wild, crazy, dark, and scary rides — and are at least 44 inches tall — give it a try. And be sure to say hello to the yeti for us!

#1 RIDE READER PLEASER

WILD DARK SCARY

YOU MUST BE AT LEAST 44 INCHES TALL TO RIDE EXPEDITION EVEREST.

Kali River Rapids

This is one of the wettest and wildest rides in Walt Disney World. (Don't bother trying to pick a dry seat on the raft, because there aren't any.) It begins as a peaceful trip through a rainforest. But things don't stay calm for very long. The raft bumps along down the river, spinning and turning every time it hits a wall.

Along the way you catch a glimpse of how logging (cutting down trees for lumber) can destroy the rainforest. Don't be scared if you see a fire — that's just part of the ride. You avoid the burning logs, but will you really go under that big waterfall? We won't tell. But you might want to bring a towel, just in case.

WILD

WET

YOU MUST BE AT LEAST 38 INCHES TALL TO RIDE KALI RIVER RAPIDS.

HOT TIP!

Want to keep your stuff dry while you ride Kali River Rapids? Leave it in a locker near the ride's entrance. Lockers are free for up to 2 hours.

FP+

UP! A Great Bird Adventure

Live birds are the stars of this show in the Asia section of the park. They swoop and soar and do amazing tricks. They are joined by everyone's favorite Wilderness Explorer, Russell, and his furry friend, Dug.

The show is fun for all ages and presented several times a day. It lasts about 25 minutes. Don't leave right away — sometimes a handler will bring a bird out to meet guests.

The high-flying action happens in the Anandapur (say: *ah-NAHN-dah-purr*) theater. The seating area is covered, but it does not have air-conditioning.

This show was on pause in 2021. Will it be offered during your visit? Ask a parent to check *disneyworld.com* for updates.

FP+

WHO AM I?

- I have a long tail.
- I wear a Fez hat.
- Aladdin is my pal!

Answer: Abu

Pandora — The World of Avatar

Disney's Animal Kingdom has a special land called Pandora — The World of Avatar. It is a beautiful area that celebrates nature and all animal life. It has floating mountains, bridges, waterfalls, and plants. Many of the plants glow at night! The area has two attractions to enjoy: Na'vi River Journey and Avatar Flight of Passage.

Avatar Flight of Passage FP+

Who said you need wings to fly? Just climb aboard a Mountain Banshee and soar over Pandora in this exciting thrill ride. It is sure to please most kids — especially the daredevils. In case you are wondering: A Mountain Banshee is a flying creature that looks like a dragon. It is also known as an *Ikran* (say: EEK-*rahn*).

Meet your avatar

Mountain Banshees don't like humans — that's why all guests need avatars (AV-*eh-tars*). Your avatar will ride the Ikran's back while you sit on something that's like a motorcycle seat. Everyone wears 3-D glasses, too.

Fly, Ikran, fly!

As the adventure begins, the powerful creature zooms through the air — and you're along for the ride. Hang on! Most kids agree that this is an amazing experience — so it is very popular. Get a Fastpass if you can. If heights or motion make you feel uncomfortable, you should skip this attraction.

WILD

LOUD

YOU MUST BE AT LEAST 44 INCHES TALL TO RIDE AVATAR FLIGHT OF PASSAGE.

READER REVIEW

Flight of Passage is the best ride in the world! It feels like you are actually riding on a living creature. My dream to temporarily run away from Earth and ride a Banshee has come true!

— Kathleen (age 12), Normal, IL

Na'vi River Journey FP+

DARK

The Na'vi River Journey is a peaceful boat ride through a dark, glowing jungle. As you float on a mysterious river, be sure to notice all the details. Expect to see interesting creatures and glowing plants. You'll also see (and hear) an Audio-Animatronics character called the Shaman of Song. She is gigantic! This journey is a nice way to take a cool break on a hot day.

The Oasis

The Oasis is a small, green area at the front of Animal Kingdom. It is a lot like an oasis in a desert. It has pretty plants and flowing water. It's also home to some of the park's coolest critters. There's wildlife to discover on both sides of the Oasis. You can check out one side as you enter and the other side as you leave the park.

The Oasis Exhibits

The Oasis is home to many animals. Some are easier to spot than others. They hang out in areas called exhibits. That means they are there for you to admire. You may spy creatures that fly and some who swim — and some who do both! You should keep an eye out for a giant anteater, boar, barking deer, and wallabies. Some of the animals are shy and like to hide. Others play in the open. Be sure to have a camera ready.

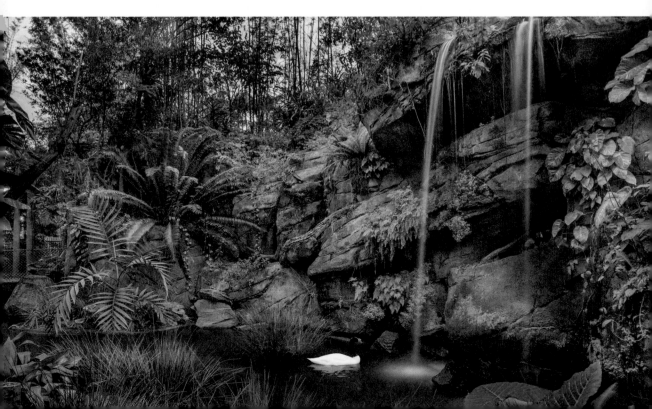

Entertainment

Animal Kingdom has some very talented performers. Some walk on two legs, while others walk on four — or eight. There are usually lots of shows every day. You can read about some of them below.

Many shows were on pause in 2021. Will they be back for 2022? Ask a parent to check *disneyworld.com* for updates.

Donald's Dino-Bash

Donald Duck just heard some amazing news. Some of his ancestors were dinosaurs! And that has put him in a party mood. Head to DinoLand to help him celebrate. You may also have a chance to meet Chip, Dale, Daisy, Goofy, Pluto, and other Disney friends — and join dance parties throughout the day.

Bollywood Beats

Put your dancing shoes on and head to Asia for an exciting musical show. Bollywood Beats invites guests to join in all kinds of dances from India. Some of the dances are very old, others are new — and they are all interactive.

African Entertainment

Drummers may perform in Harambe during the day. There's a covered area where you can listen to them and escape the blazing sun.

Pandora Drummers

To hear musicians bang giant drums, visit the Valley of Mo'ara in Pandora — The World of Avatar. Each show is a Na'vi drum ceremony. It's a celebration of the Pandora spirit.

Pandora Rangers

There is a 10-foot-tall robot roaming the Valley of Mo'ara. It is piloted by a human (who is inside a mechanical suit). As the robot explores Pandora, the pilot talks to park guests. Together, everyone learns about the power of nature.

Tree of Life Awakenings

After dark, the Tree of Life wakes up covered in pretty lights and pictures of animals. The colorful shows takes place every ten minutes. The show covers the Tree of Life on all sides — so it's hard to miss. Watching this show is a nice way to end the day.

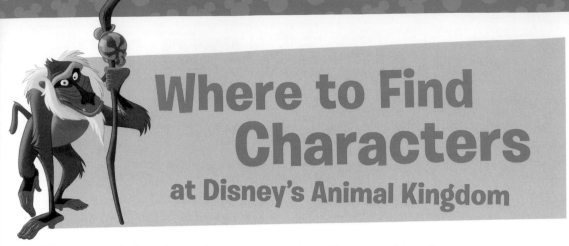

Where to Find Characters
at Disney's Animal Kingdom

It's fun to search for Disney characters at Animal Kingdom. **Adventurers Outpost** on Discovery Island is a good place to find Mickey and Minnie.

Flik may hang out by **Creature Comforts**. Look for Donald, Daisy, Goofy, Pluto, Chip, Dale, Launchpad McQuack, and Scrooge McDuck at **Donald's Dino-Bash** in DinoLand U.S.A. Timon, Rafiki, Russell, and Dug wave hi to fans on **Discovery Island**. You may get to see Kevin, too. Pocahontas may visit Discovery Island (at the Discovery Island Trails).

Disney characters love a good photo op. When it's safe for folks to be close, Disney friends will stand near you. Until then, characters are happy to pose in the background of selfies. So have your camera ready!

Details may change in 2022.

TIPS

Animal Kingdom can get very warm, especially in the summer months. Head for Festival of the Lion King, Finding Nemo — The Musical, Kali River Rapids, or Rafiki's Planet Watch to cool off. And don't forget to drink lots of water.

Go to Avatar Flight of Passage, Expedition Everest, Dinosaur, and Kali River Rapids early — before they get too crowded. Use Fastpass if it is offered.

On the Kilimanjaro Safaris ride, look at the chart over your head. The pictures will show which animals you're about to see.

Can't find your parents? Ask the closest Disney Cast Member for help (a park worker wearing a name tag).

It doesn't really matter what time you get to the Kilimanjaro Safaris ride — the animals are there all day long.

It's Tough to Be a Bug is very scary to some kids (especially those who don't like the dark, or get spooked by insects). In the show, bugs seem to shoot quills and stinky smells, giant spiders dangle from the ceiling, and creepy critters seem to scamper under the seats. If you get scared during the show, it's okay to grab your parent and leave early.

It's fun to see how many animals you can find carved into The Tree of Life. Some folks use binoculars.

Find Mickey and Minnie at the Adventurers Outpost on Discovery Island. Bring a smart phone or camera.

There's a big painting at the entrance of Conservation Station at Rafiki's Planet Watch. It's filled with animal images and Hidden Mickeys. How many can you find?

Stash your stuff in a locker before riding Kali River Rapids — unless you don't mind if it gets wet.

Attraction Ratings

COOL
(Check it out!)

- The Oasis (the area inside the park entrance)

- Affection Section (at Rafiki's Planet Watch)

- TriceraTop Spin

- Na'vi River Journey

- Donald's Dino-Bash

- UP! A Great Bird Adventure

VERY COOL
(Don't miss!)

- The Boneyard playground

- It's Tough to Be a Bug!

- Maharajah Jungle Trek

- Gorilla Falls Exploration Trail

- Finding Nemo — The Musical

- Drawn to Magic (at Rafiki's Planet Watch)

COOLEST
(See at least twice!)

- Expedition Everest

- Avatar Flight of Passage

- Kilimanjaro Safaris

- Kali River Rapids

- Festival of the Lion King

- Dinosaur

YOUR FAVORITE ANIMAL KINGDOM ATTRACTIONS

_____   _____

_____   _____

_____

Everything Else in the World

No matter what you're interested in — water fun, sports, or animals — Walt Disney World has enough to make every minute of your vacation a blast. After you visit the theme parks, there's still so much to do. There are water parks, speedy boats to rent, horses to ride, fish to catch, and lots of neat shopping spots.

If you are into sports, you may want to check out the ESPN Wide World of Sports Complex, rent a bicycle, or try some mini golf. To test your detective skills, join one of Walt Disney World's special scavenger hunts.

In this chapter, you can read up on all the extra activities and find out about hotels and restaurants at Walt Disney World. Then you can help your family decide where to stay, where to eat, and what to do when you are not at the theme parks.

Waters of the World

It's easy to get wet, stay cool, and have fun at Walt Disney World. That's because it's a water wonderland. Choose a water park or swim in your hotel pool. (If you are younger than age 14 and you want to visit a water park, you must go with a guest who is older than 14.)

HOT TIP!

Typhoon Lagoon was closed for most of 2021. Will it be open during your visit in 2022? Ask a parent to use the My Disney Experience app or visit *disneyworld.com* to find out.

Typhoon Lagoon

A typhoon is a powerful, wet, and windy storm. It dumps huge amounts of rain and sends objects flying through the air. This water park looks like a typhoon blew through it. There's even a boat stuck on a mountaintop! Of course, a storm didn't really put the boat there — Disney Imagineers did. They also put in pools, water slides, and a raft ride.

Catch the wave

The big pool here is like a small ocean. It has 6-foot waves! There are speed slides to try, too. In the mood for a big thrill? If you are at least 48 inches tall, try Crush 'n' Gusher. It's like a water roller coaster. For a calmer experience, you can hop into a tube and float along a lazy river. There is also a special area just for younger kids — Ketchakiddee Creek. It has small slides and other games. You must be 48 inches or shorter to play in Ketchakiddee Creek (and have a grown-up with you).

Miss Adventure Falls

There's an exciting new ride in town. Miss Adventure Falls is a wild water ride for the whole family — up to four people can travel in a raft. It is the longest ride ever built at a Disney World water park. Hold on tight! During the 2-minute trip, you will spy lots of sparkly things. Keep your eyes out for a treasure-hunting parrot.

Blizzard Beach

Would you wear a swimsuit to a snow-covered mountain? Probably not. But you should wear one to Blizzard Beach. It looks like a place to ski, but it's really a splashy water park. So don't worry if you can't ski. Nobody skis down the mountains here. They slide!

Reach the peak

Like a real ski resort, the action centers around a mountain. In this case, it is Mount Gushmore. To get to the top, you can take a chairlift. The ride gives you a great view of the park. The scariest slide on the mountain is Summit Plummet. It begins 120 feet in the air, on a platform that looks like a ski jump. It drops you down a steep slide at about 60 miles per hour. That's faster than many cars go on the highway! You can ride Summit Plummet if you are at least 48 inches tall.

Slip-sliding away

There are plenty of ways to slide down the mountain. Tube slides, body slides, and inner tube rides can keep you busy all day long. It's fun to splash in the wave pool, too. For preteens, there's Ski Patrol Training Camp, with its "iceberg" obstacle course and ropes for swinging into the water. Tike's Peak is a special place for younger kids. It has slides and a snow-castle fountain play area.

READER TIP

"Go to a water park early in the day — when it's hot and crowded at the theme parks. Then you can return to the theme park when it cools down in the evening."

— David (age 14),
Calabasas, CA

HOT TIP!

Bring water shoes to Walt Disney World water parks. That way, you won't burn your feet when you walk around. The ground can get super hot in the summer months!

Fort Wilderness

Fort Wilderness is tucked away in a woodsy area of Walt Disney World. (It isn't really a fort. It's a campground.) You can stay the night or come for a day. There are tennis and volleyball courts, and a marina with lots of boats. You could spend days here and not run out of things to do. If you have time, stop at the pony farm or ride in a boat on Bay Lake and Seven Seas Lagoon.

Pony Farm

There is a small farm at Fort Wilderness. It's a short walk from Pioneer Hall. There is no charge to visit the farm, but it costs about $9 for a pony ride. Be sure to bring a grown-up with you. If you don't want to ride a pony, you can still stop by and say hello. Most visitors think a trip to the farm is a fun way to spend some time away from the parks.

YOU MUST BE LESS THAN 48 INCHES TALL TO RIDE A PONY AT WALT DISNEY WORLD.

More Fort Wilderness Fun

Fort Wilderness offers lots of other things to do. You can rent a canoe for a trip along a canal. Or you can rent a bicycle and explore the trails. At the Tri-Circle-D Ranch, you can visit the horses that pull the trolleys in the Magic Kingdom. (The horses live in a big barn near Pioneer Hall.)

Kids older than 9 can take a trail ride on horseback. With a parent, kids can also enjoy a wagon ride, do some fishing, or roast marshmallows at a campfire with Chip and Dale.

Sports

Kids who like sports can find plenty of ways to keep active at Walt Disney World. You can rent boats and bikes at a resort, or play mini golf on a themed course. To see athletes at work, visit ESPN Wide World of Sports Complex. Read on to find out how.

ESPN Wide World of Sports Complex

Sports nuts might enjoy a visit to this place. It has facilities for every sport you can imagine. You can spend a day watching some amateur sporting events.

This place was closed in 2021. When it opens up again, tickets to the complex will cost about $14 for kids ages 3 to 9 and about $19 for anyone 10 or older. If you want to attend a special event, you have to buy tickets ahead of time. A parent should call 407-939-4263 for tickets.

Motorboats

Walt Disney World is home to speedy little motorboats. The zippy boats go fast and the ride can be bumpy — especially if you drive over a wave made by another boat. So hang on tight. And drive carefully — there is a lot of traffic out there. Stay far away from other watercraft.

Boats are usually available at WDW hotels — but they were not offered in 2021. Will they be open during your visit? Ask a grown-up to visit *disneyworld.com* to find out.

Guests must be at least 12 years old and 5 feet tall to drive a motorboat. Details may change.

Miniature Golf

Even if you have never held a golf club before, you may enjoy mini golf. It's fun to play and full of surprises.

Fantasia Gardens

If you've seen the classic movie *Fantasia*, you will know how this miniature golf course got its name. Where else would you find hippos on tiptoe, dancing mushrooms, or xylophone stairs?

The holes are grouped by musical themes. At the Dance of the Hours hole, watch the hippopotamus standing on an alligator. If you hit a golf ball through the gator's mouth, the hippo dances!

The cost is about $12 to play one round for kids ages 3 to 9 and about $14 for anyone 10 or older.

Disney's Winter Summerland

Sometimes Santa Claus needs a vacation. Just like you, he has picked Walt Disney World as the perfect place to have fun!

As the story goes, Santa and his helpers built these mini-golf courses as a place to relax and enjoy the sun. That's why one looks like a beach, with sand castles and surfboards on it. But then the elves got homesick, so they built a second course that reminded them of the North Pole. Everything looks like it is covered in snow. There are even igloos, jolly snow people, and holes for ice fishing.

For a bit of a challenge, try the summer course. It's a little harder than the winter course. Santa is snoozing at one of the trickiest holes. You have to hit the ball across his belly without waking him up. The winter holes offer surprises, too.

To play on one course, it costs about $12 for kids ages 3 to 9 and about $14 for folks age 10 or older. This course was closed when this book was made. Will it be open during your visit? Ask a parent to check *disneyworld.com* for updates.

Scavenger Hunts

If you are a fan of the tales told by Walt Disney World's shows and rides, you will probably enjoy these special tours. Each one makes you feel as if you are part of the story.

Many tours were on pause in 2021. Will they be offered in 2022? Ask a parent to visit *disneyworld.com* for updates.

Family Magic Tour

This program is fun for the whole family. Parents and kids can join in a themed scavenger hunt through the Magic Kingdom. Guests search for the answers to different clues that lead to the missing item.

If you go on this two-hour tour, be sure to wear sneakers — you will be doing lots of walking! The cost is about $39 for each person age 3 and over. Parents can use the My Disney Experience app or website, or call 407-WDW-TOUR (939-8687) to make reservations.

Pirate Adventure

Did you know there is pirates' treasure buried at Walt Disney World? Some is hidden somewhere around Crescent Lake. Every morning, a cruise for kids sails out from the Yacht Club resort in search of it. The experience is called the Albatross Treasure Cruise.

The Caribbean Beach resort has a special pirate adventure, too. Do you think you are up to the challenge of a treasure hunt? The captain of the ship will give you a map and clues to help you on your way. During the journey, all junior pirates get to enjoy a drink and a snack.

You will have two hours to find the hidden treasure. If you do, it is yours to keep! Cruises take place each morning and are for kids ages 4 to 12. The cost is about $49 per child. Cruises happen every day, but they may be canceled if the weather is bad. To make reservations, a parent can call 407-WDW-PLAY (939-7529) or visit *www.mydisneyexperience.com*.

Disney Springs

Disney Springs is a great place to visit on a non-park day. It has shops, games, movies, restaurants, and much more. There are areas to explore and lots to discover — like life-like dinosaurs and cars that are also boats. Some spots offer live entertainment. There are four neighborhoods at Disney Springs: Town Center, Marketplace, The West Side, and The Landing. Town Center is a big outdoor shopping mall. Read on to learn about the other areas.

The West Side

This zone has places to shop, eat, bowl, watch a movie, and hear live music. It also has a big balloon that takes guests for rides in the sky. (You will need a ticket and a grown-up to ride with you.) There's a new stage show, too. Drawn to Life is a celebration of Disney animation.

Marketplace

Searching for a souvenir? Head straight to the Marketplace. There are lots of shops there.

One place that kids enjoy is World of Disney. It's a shop with Disney-themed goodies. Nearby, you can dig for fossils in a dino-themed restaurant or check out giant statues made out of LEGOs. They are super cool!

The Landing

This neighborhood has waterside shops and snack spots. It's also where the Amphicars are. They are cars that float! It usually costs about $125 per cruise.

HOT TIP!

Many of the activities in Disney Springs were on pause when this book was made. What will be open when you visit? To find out, ask a parent to use the My Disney Experience mobile app or visit *disneyworld.com*.

Electrical Water Pageant

Have you ever seen a parade on a lake? Now is your chance. The Electrical Water Pageant is Disney's floating parade. The pageant made its magical debut in October 1971. It was part of the grand opening of the Polynesian Village Resort. Walt Disney World was 3 weeks old at the time.

Above the sea

The water parade takes place on The Seven Seas Lagoon (the lake next to the Magic Kingdom) and on Bay Lake (behind the Contemporary resort hotel). The nightly show has thousands of sparkling lights on connected floats. The floats have screens that show King Triton and other sea creatures — turtles, sea horses, an octopus, and a sea serpent. It's all set to Disney music. The pageant may be canceled when the weather is windy or stormy.

The end of the parade is a tribute to America. That's when the lights become flags and stars. The finale has a patriotic music medley, too. If you know the words to "You're a Grand Old Flag" and "Yankee Doodle Dandy," feel free to sing along.

Catch it if you can!

You can see the Electrical Water Pageant from many places around Bay Lake and the Seven Seas Lagoon. Each water parade lasts about 15 minutes. Start times may vary. Here is the schedule:

- Polynesian Village Resort — about 9 P.M.
- Grand Floridian Resort — about 9:15 P.M.
- Wilderness Lodge — about 9:30 P.M.
- Disney's Fort Wilderness Resort and Campground — about 9:45 P.M.
- Contemporary Resort — about 10:10 P.M. (When the Magic Kingdom's fireworks take place at 10 P.M., the Water Pageant begins soon after the fireworks end.)
- On nights when the Magic Kingdom is open late, the show takes place right outside the park entrance — about 10:35 P.M.

Walt Disney World Resort Hotels

There are more than 25 hotels at Walt Disney World. There are so many hotel rooms that you could stay in a different one every night for 68 years! Just like the rides at the parks, each of the resorts has its own special theme. And all of the hotels are fun to stay at. But it can be nice to visit, too. So if you have time, you might want to stop by some of them. You can have a snack or just enjoy the Disney atmosphere.

Resorts near the Magic Kingdom

Contemporary

This was the first-ever Walt Disney World hotel. It looked very modern when it was built in 1971. And it still looks cool fifty years later! When the hotel opened, it had a talking elevator and a monorail station right in the middle of it. It still has the monorail, plus a fun pool and Chef Mickey's — a place to have a meal and see Mickey Mouse and his pals.

CONTEMPORARY TIP

In the center of the resort is a 3-sided mural that's 90 feet tall. There are colorful pictures of children and animals all over it. One of the goats has five legs. See how long it takes you to find it!

Fort Wilderness

Stay in a camper, tent, or cabin at this pretty campground. This resort has many activities. You can go for a wagon ride, visit a pony farm, or take a trip through the woods on a horse. At night, Chip and Dale sometimes roast marshmallows by a campfire. This is also home to a popular dinner show called the Hoop-Dee-Doo Musical Revue.

FORT WILDERNESS TIP

The friendly horses that pull trolleys in the Magic Kingdom live in a stable at Fort Wilderness. You can visit for free — and maybe even see them getting new shoes from the blacksmith.

Wilderness Lodge

With its log columns and totem poles, this hotel looks like a national park from the American Northwest. The fireplaces and rocking chairs in the main building make you feel right at home. There is an indoor stream and a bridge. Outside, there is an erupting geyser and a pool. There are so many Hidden Mickeys here that there's a contest to see how many you can find.

WILDERNESS LODGE TIP
Look for the "Proterozoic Fossils and Minerals" display. It's a key to the rocky strata of the giant Grand Canyon fireplace in the main lobby.

Polynesian Village

The plants and trees at this hotel make it look like a tropical island. The greenery and cheery colors in the main building make the setting seem real even when you're indoors. There's a pool that looks like it is made from lava from a volcano, and a beach to relax on. The WDW monorail makes a stop here, too.

POLYNESIAN VILLAGE TIP
Grab a snack (and your family) and have a picnic on or near the beach. Then enjoy the fireworks over the Magic Kingdom — the show's music plays all around you! (Fireworks may not be offered during your visit to WDW.)

Grand Floridian

This hotel looks like a huge mansion from the early 1900s. At first, it seems to be for adults, but it's also fun for kids. There may be activities like storytelling and crafts. Or you can sit in a comfy chair and listen to a band play in the lobby. There are two pools: one is surrounded by roses and the other has a waterfall. There's an Alice in Wonderland splash zone, too. The monorail stops here.

GRAND FLORIDIAN TIP
In November and December, the Grand Floridian is home to a giant gingerbread house. It is made with real gingerbread and so big that a few grown-up people can fit inside!

PHOTO BY JILL SAFRO

THE MONORAIL

The monorail connects the Magic Kingdom park with the Contemporary, Polynesian Village, and Grand Floridian resorts. It's also a great way to travel from the Magic Kingdom park to EPCOT. Just switch monorail trains when you get to the Transportation and Ticket Center. (The Transportation and Ticket Center is also called the T.T.C.)

Resorts near EPCOT and Disney's Hollywood Studios

BoardWalk

This hotel is designed to look the way Atlantic City, New Jersey, once did. Just like on an old-fashioned boardwalk, there are games and snack stands here for everyone to enjoy. You can rent a special bicycle built for four. And you can splash in a pool zone that looks like an amusement park.

BOARDWALK TIP

In the lobby, there is a crystal globe under the golden chandelier. The globe is a time capsule! It's set to be opened this year — as part of Walt Disney World's 50th anniversary celebration. Be sure to stop and take a peek.

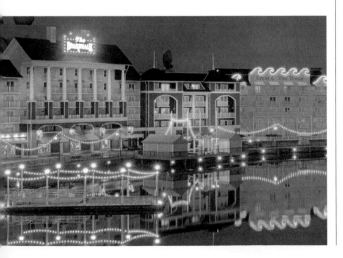

Port Orleans — French Quarter

Details at this hotel make it look as if it is in New Orleans, Louisiana. There's a long river and a cool pool. The pool has a water slide that looks like a sea serpent's tongue.

PORT ORLEANS — FRENCH QUARTER TIP

After taking a dip in the French Quarter pool, you may want to visit the pool at Port Orleans Riverside. You can walk or take a Walt Disney World bus. Be sure to take your parents with you!

Port Orleans — Riverside

This hotel's buildings look like mansions and country homes from the Old South. The food court is designed after a cotton mill, and it has a water-wheel that is 30 feet tall. The pool is on Ol' Man Island, an area that was inspired by the story of Tom Sawyer.

PORT ORLEANS — RIVERSIDE TIP

If you like to fish, head down to the Fishin' Hole at Ol' Man Island. The recreation area has fishing poles to rent and bait to buy.

Caribbean Beach

Happy and colorful, this hotel looks like resorts on some Caribbean islands. You can have fun in the sun all day at its pools and playgrounds. A bunch of the rooms here have a pirate theme. And there is a cool, interactive splash area and slide at the pool.

CARIBBEAN BEACH TIP

The hotel has a bike path that circles a lake. It's more than a mile long! Bikes can be rented at the marina.

Riviera

Walt Disney loved traveling through Europe. The Riviera hotel is based on what he saw during his visits. There are bubbling fountains, quiet gardens, and beautiful artwork to enjoy.

RIVIERA TIP

There's lots of outdoor fun to be had here. Kids love the interactive splash zone by the pool. You can play bocce, lawn chess, and other games, too.

Old Key West

The town houses that make up this resort have all the comforts of home. The palm trees and sunny design make it a warm and welcoming place. And the pool has an awesome slide.

OLD KEY WEST TIP

Kids of all ages enjoy the crafts and games at Community Hall. The wet and wild games at the main swimming pool are lots of fun, too.

READER TIP

"The TVs in Disney hotel rooms have a channel that is all about Walt Disney World. Don't miss it!"

— Nicholas (age 9), Mount Pleasant, SC

Pop Century Resort

The twentieth century might be over, but it is hard to forget when you visit this hotel. Giant pieces of art (like old cell phones and jukeboxes) decorate the buildings. The hotel pays tribute to each decade from the 1950s to the 1990s.

POP CENTURY TIP

On hot days, you can cool off by splashing around in the hotel's interactive fountains.

Saratoga Springs Resort

This hotel is designed to look like upstate New York in the late 1800s. There are lots of pretty gardens to look at. But the best views come from a special lakeside spot. From there you can see the lights of Disney Springs. The pools here are a blast!

SARATOGA SPRINGS TIP

The pool area has a special water-spray play area with lots of squirting fountains. It's just for kids.

Yacht and Beach Club

These hotels are meant to look like the homes near the beaches of Massachusetts. Even the pool makes it feel as if you're at the beach — the bottom is covered with sand.

YACHT AND BEACH CLUB TIP

Pack walking shoes. One of the best parts about staying here is that you can walk to EPCOT, Disney's Hollywood Studios, and BoardWalk.

Swan and Dolphin

You can't miss the dolphin and swan statues that sit on top of these hotels — they are huge. There's a lot to do at the Swan and Dolphin. The pool area is a ton of fun. And you can walk or take a FriendShip boat to EPCOT, Disney's Hollywood Studios, and the BoardWalk resort from the hotels.

SWAN AND DOLPHIN TIP

There are 250 swan and dolphin statues at this resort. Some are big, but some are very small. See how many you can spot.

PHOTO BY JILL SAFRO

Art of Animation

This resort celebrates animation. And if you are a fan of *Finding Nemo*, *The Little Mermaid*, *The Lion King*, or *Cars*, you are going to love it here. Be sure to look up — there are tons of giant character statues. Super cool!

ART OF ANIMATION TIP

Kids love the pools at this resort. Don't miss the splash zone in the *Finding Nemo* Courtyard. It's a great place to have fun with a younger brother or sister.

Resorts near Disney's Animal Kingdom

Coronado Springs

This hotel celebrates the daring spirit of Spanish explorers, artists, and writers. The buildings are the color of clay. The pool looks like an ancient pyramid, with a slide that passes under a spitting jaguar. Beside it is a playground with ancient treasures waiting to be discovered.

CORONADO SPRINGS TIP

The resort has a play area called The Explorers Zone. It is designed to look like Aztec ruins. Kids ages 2 to 12 may enjoy its slides, jungle gym, and dig site.

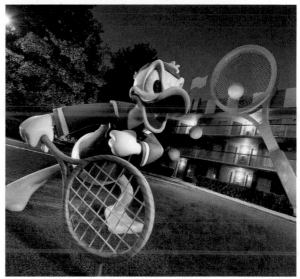

All-Star Resorts

There are three All-Star resorts, and each one of them has a theme — sports, music, or movies. It's easy to tell which All-Star you are visiting because they have giant icons that are bigger than the buildings. At All-Star Music, look for big cowboy boots. A huge football helmet means you are at All-Star Sports. And when you see a 38-foot-tall Buzz Lightyear, there's no doubt you are at All-Star Movies.

ALL-STAR TIP

There are a whole lot of Hidden Mickeys to hunt for! Start your search at the main statue in each of the resorts.

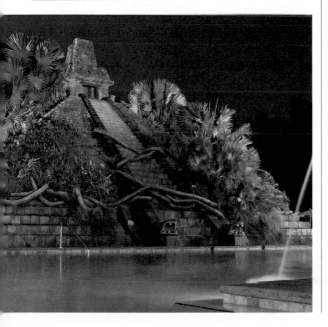

Animal Kingdom Lodge

Creatures like giraffes, zebras, gazelles, and beautiful birds live near this hotel — and they are all real. The trees and animals make it seem as if the resort is set in an African savanna. A giant mud fireplace and thatched roofs add to the feeling that you really are in Africa.

ANIMAL KINGDOM LODGE TIP

Almost all of the rooms at Animal Kingdom Lodge have good views of the animals. But if you want an even closer look, remember to bring some binoculars from home.

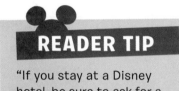

READER TIP

"If you stay at a Disney hotel, be sure to ask for a wake-up call. It is usually Mickey Mouse or Stitch."

— Raquel (age 7), Miami, FL

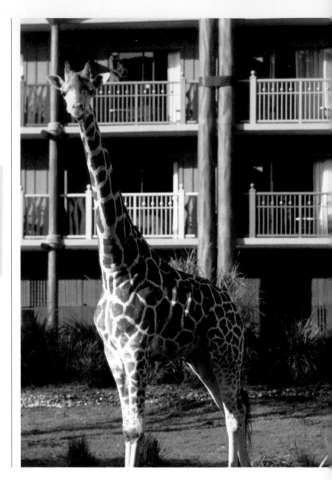

MOVIES UNDER THE STARS

There are lots of fun things for kids to enjoy at Walt Disney World resorts. One of them is called Movies Under the Stars. On most nights, a Disney film is shown outdoors. Sometimes there is a campfire and marshmallow roast before the show. You can get a movie schedule at your hotel's front desk. (The movie may be moved indoors or canceled if the weather is bad.)

HOT TIP!

Movies Under the Stars are extra special at Disney's Fort Wilderness resort. Chip and Dale often stop by to say hello before the movie begins!

Restaurants

Eating at Walt Disney World can be as much fun as riding Splash Mountain (well, almost as much fun!). Here are our ideas for the best spots in each theme park to head to for your favorite foods.

HOT TIP!

There are lots of healthy and delicious menu choices for kids at Disney World. Just look for this symbol on the menu.

MAGIC KINGDOM

CANDY AND CRISPIE TREATS . . . . Main Street Confectionery

CHICKEN NUGGETS . . . . Cosmic Ray's Starlight Cafe

COOKIES . . . . Main Street Confectionery

FRUIT . . . . Liberty Square Market

HAMBURGERS . . . . Cosmic Ray's Starlight Cafe

HOT DOGS . . . . Casey's Corner

ICE CREAM . . . . Plaza Ice Cream Parlor

LEFOU'S BREW (APPLE SLUSH DRINK) . . . . Gaston's Tavern

MACARONI AND CHEESE . . . . Columbia Harbour House

PIZZA . . . . Pinocchio Village Haus

PRETZELS . . . . Fantasyland Pretzel Stand (in Storybook Circus)

SMOOTHIES . . . . Main Street Bakery

TURKEY LEGS . . . . Frontierland Turkey Leg Cart

VEGGIE BURGERS . . . . Cosmic Ray's Starlight Cafe

EPCOT
Best Places for Favorite Foods

CANDY AND COOKIES . . . . Karamell-Küche (in Germany)

CHEESEBURGERS . . . . Regal Eagle (in the American Adventure)

HOT DOGS . . . . Fife and Drum Tavern (in the American Adventure)

EGG ROLLS . . . . Lotus Blossom Cafe (in China)

FRUIT . . . . Sunshine Seasons (in The Land)

ICE CREAM . . . . L'Artisan des Glaces (in France)

JUMBO PRETZELS . . . . The Pretzel Wagon (in Germany)

MACARONI AND CHEESE . . . . Sunshine Seasons (in The Land)

PASTA WITH TOMATO SAUCE . . . . Via Napoli (in Italy)

PASTRIES . . . . Les Halles Boulangerie Patisserie (in France)

PEANUT BUTTER & JELLY SANDWICHES . . . . . . Sunshine Seasons (in The Land)

PIZZA . . . . Via Napoli (in Italy)

TACOS . . . . La Cantina de San Angel (in Mexico)

TURKEY LEG . . . . Fife and Drum Tavern (in the American Adventure)

DISNEY'S HOLLYWOOD STUDIOS
Best Places for Favorite Foods

CHICKEN AND WAFFLES . . . . The Backlot Express

CHICKEN NOODLE SOUP . . . . Sci-Fi Dine-In Theater

CHICKEN NUGGETS . . . . ABC Commissary

FRUIT . . . . Anaheim Produce (in Sunset Ranch Market)

GRILLED CHEESE . . . . Woody's Lunch Box (in Toy Story Land)

HAMBURGERS . . . . Backlot Express

HOT DOGS . . . . Fairfax Fare (in Sunset Ranch Market)

ICE CREAM . . . . Hollywood Scoops (in Sunset Ranch Market)

MACARONI AND CHEESE . . . . Hollywood and Vine

MILK SHAKES . . . . 50's Prime Time Cafe

PEANUT BUTTER & JELLY SANDWICHES . . . . ABC Commissary

PIZZA . . . . PizzeRizzo

SMOOTHIES . . . . Trolley Car Cafe

SPAGHETTI . . . . Mama Melrose's Ristorante Italiano

HOT TIP!

Most Disney restaurants have special meals for kids. Just ask!

DISNEY'S ANIMAL KINGDOM
Best Places for Favorite Foods

BARBECUED RIBS AND CHICKEN . . . . Flame Tree Barbecue

CANDY . . . . Chester and Hester's Dinosaur Treasures

CHICKEN NUGGETS AND FRIES . . . . Restaurantosaurus

COOKIES . . . . Kusafiri Coffee Shop and Bakery

CORN DOGS . . . . Famous Sausages (in Harambe Market)

EGG ROLLS . . . . Yak and Yeti Local Food Cafes

FRUIT . . . . Harambe Fruit Market

GRILLED CHEESE . . . . Rainforest Cafe

HAMBURGERS . . . . Restaurantosaurus

HOT DOGS . . . . Restaurantosaurus

ICE CREAM . . . . Anandapur Ice Cream Truck

PIZZA . . . . Pizzafari

SMOOTHIES . . . . Creature Comforts

VEGGIE BURGERS . . . . Rainforest Cafe

Eating with Disney Characters

Kids of all ages enjoy eating with the characters. It's one of the best ways to see your favorite Disney stars. Bring a camera because the characters are also happy to pose for photos. They love to be in the background of your selfies!

Each of the theme parks has at least one restaurant that invites the characters over. Many of the resorts have character meals, too. They are very popular, so no matter which restaurant your family chooses, it's a good idea to make reservations far ahead of time. Ask a parent to call 407-WDW-DINE (939-3463).

Character meals aren't fun just because you get to see the characters. They are also special because the food is yummy! Picky eaters may enjoy family-style meals — with so much to choose from, there's something for everyone.

Many character meals were on pause in 2021. Will they return in 2022? Ask a parent to visit *disneyworld.com* to find out!

Dinner Shows

Hoop-Dee-Doo Musical Revue

Entertainers sing, dance, and tell jokes while you chow down on chicken, ribs, and veggies. If you go, be prepared to clap your hands, stomp your feet, and sing along. The jokes are silly, but everyone always has a good time. The food is tasty, too. That's probably why the Hoop-Dee-Doo is the most popular dinner show in all of Walt Disney World!

The Spirit of Aloha

Aloha! That means "hello" (and "good-bye") in Hawaiian. You will hear it a lot at this show. Performers do the hula and other dances while servers dish out Polynesian food. (This show may change soon.)

For details, a parent can call 407-WDW-DINE (939-3463), or visit *www.mydisneyexperience.com*.

Dinner shows may not be offered in all of 2022.

MAGICAL MEMORIES

The fun doesn't have to end when your vacation does.
Use these pages to preserve your Disney memories.

These are the people I vacationed with:

I arrived at Walt Disney World on:

_____
Month / Day / Year

I stayed for _____ days.

On my first day at Walt Disney World I went to:

The name of our hotel was:

My usual bedtime is _____ o'clock.

During my trip, the latest I went to bed was _____ o'clock!

The earliest I woke up was _____ o'clock.

I traveled to Walt Disney World by:

☐ car ☐ train
☐ bus ☐ ship
☐ plane ☐ flying carpet

If I were a Disney Imagineer, this is the ride I would make:

This attraction was not what I expected:

It surprised me because:

Draw your favorite Disney character here:

The weather at Walt Disney World was:

☐ sunny   ☐ rainy

☐ cloudy   ☐ cold

☐ windy

The scariest ride I went on was:

Tape a WDW receipt here.

My least favorite ride was:

I didn't like it because:

My favorite ride was:

I went on it _____ times.

Building a theme park was Walt Disney's dream. This is one of my dreams:

Vacations aren't just fun — they are educational, too. One thing I learned at Walt Disney World is:

The funniest thing that happened at Walt Disney World was:

Tape a Disney World vacation photo here:

The best Disney theme park was:

☐ Magic Kingdom

☐ Epcot

☐ Disney's Hollywood Studios

☐ Disney's Animal Kingdom

My favorite Disney restaurant was:

I ate:

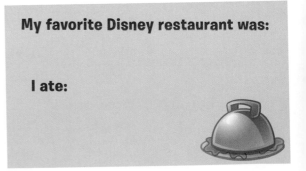

My favorite
Walt Disney World
snack is:

I found _____ Hidden Mickeys.

I met _____ characters during my vacation.
The first character I met was:

My favorite character is:

It's fun to remember a vacation with
souvenirs. One thing I brought home is:

Someday, I'll go back to Walt Disney World.
The first thing I'll do when I get there is:

ANSWERS for Page 159

1. Dumbo, the Flying Elephant = G
2. Cinderella Castle = E
3. Jungle Cruise = D
4. Mad Tea Party = F
5. Walt Disney's
   Enchanted Tiki Room = I
6. Country Bear Jamboree = A
7. Haunted Mansion = B
8. Walt Disney World Railroad = J
9. It's a Small World = C
10. Peter Pan's Flight = H

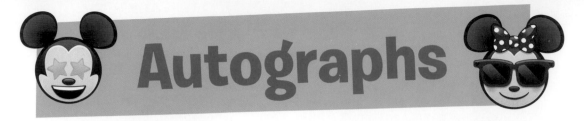

Autographs

We have all been staying apart to stay safe. That includes Disney characters. And they really missed being close to guests! They sure hope they can sign autographs in 2022. If that happens, take a pen and this book to the parks. And ask a parent to snap a photo of you with the characters you see. That will help you remember the magical moments.

MICKEY MOUSE and MINNIE MOUSE

DONALD DUCK and DAISY DUCK

ANNA and ELSA

GOOFY and PLUTO

WOODY and BUZZ

AUTOGRAPHS

AUTOGRAPHS

AUTOGRAPHS

WALT DISNEY World 50

THE WORLD'S MOST MAGICAL CELEBRATION

Happy Anniversary, Walt Disney World!

Something wonderful happened on October 1, 1971 — Walt Disney World welcomed its very first guests! And folks like you have been making memories there ever since.

This year, Walt Disney World is marking its 50th anniversary in a big way — with new experiences, snacks, and lots of surprises. The World's Most Magical Celebration started on the anniversary of Walt Disney World's opening day — October 1, 2021. And it will last 18 months! Have you ever been to a party that lasted a year and a half? Now's your chance!

So pack your bags (don't forget your camera and this book!) and get ready to celebrate 50 years of Walt Disney World magic. And if you see Mickey Mouse, be sure to say: "Happy anniversary, Mickey." That's sure to make him smile.

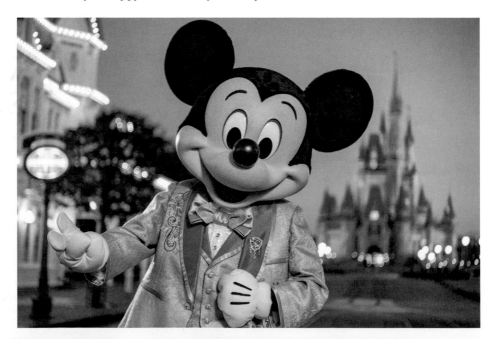

In the Beginning

On opening day, Walt Disney World had just one theme park — the Magic Kingdom! A lot has changed since October 1, 1971. And a lot has stayed the same. Mickey Mouse and his pals still love to hang out there. Fireworks still light up the night sky. And many original attractions are still making guests happy. We've listed attractions that have been here since the beginning. Can you draw a line from each name to the right photo? Good luck!

Magic Kingdom Originals

1. **Dumbo the Flying Elephant**

2. **Cinderella Castle**

3. **Jungle Cruise**

4. **Mad Tea Party**

5. **Walt Disney's Enchanted Tiki Room**

6. **Country Bear Jamboree**

7. **Haunted Mansion**

8. **Walt Disney World Railroad**

9. **It's a Small World**

10. **Peter Pan's Flight**

The answers are at the bottom of page 149!

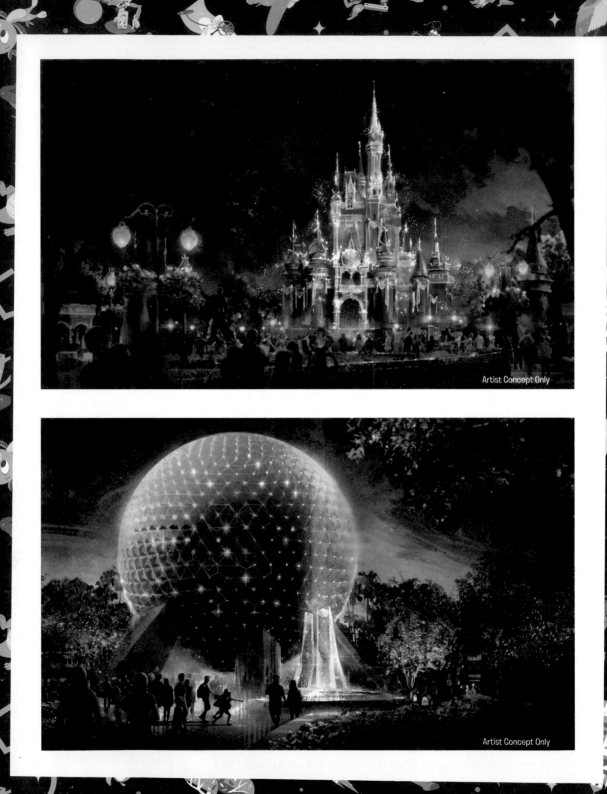

Artist Concept Only

Artist Concept Only